Homegrown Heroes

Homegrown Heroes

Local Legends in Hockey

Sam Loray

Mohammed Altaf Hussain

CONTENTS ▮

Table Of Content

Introduction
Chapter 1: The Roots of Passion
1.1. Exploration of the grassroots level of hockey in local communities
1.2. Stories of how passion for the sport is cultivated at the grassroots level
1.3. Introduction to the idea that local communities are the breeding grounds for future hockey legends

Chapter 2: Community Rinks and Outdoor Ponds
2.1. Nostalgic exploration of community rinks and outdoor ponds
2.2. Stories of how local heroes first laced up their skates in these humble settings
2.3. Discussion on the significance of these spaces in nurturing talent

Chapter 3: From Backyards to Big Leagues
3.1. Biographical sketches of selected local heroes who rose from backyard games to professional leagues
3.2. Examination of the unique skills and characteristics that set these players apart
3.3. Analysis of the impact of local mentors, coaches, and community support in their development

Chapter 4: Community Pride and Identity
4.1. Discussion on how local hockey heroes become symbols of community pride
4.2. Examination of the cultural and social impact of successful local hockey players on their communities
4.3. Stories of how hometowns rally behind their heroes, creating a sense of identity and unity

Chapter 5: Challenges and Triumphs

5.1. Exploration of the challenges faced by local hockey players in their journey to the top

5.2. Stories of triumph over adversity and the resilience displayed by these players

5.3. Examination of the role of community support during challenging times

Chapter 6: Legacy Beyond the Ice

6.1. Discussion on the lasting impact local legends have on their communities

6.2. Exploration of post-playing careers, coaching, and mentorship by these players

6.3. Analysis of the lasting legacy and inspiration they provide to aspiring young players

Chapter 7: Contextual investigations

7.1. In-depth studies of specific local legends and their contributions

7.2. Exploration of their playing style, achievements, and community involvement

7.3. Personal anecdotes and interviews with players, coaches, and community members

Introduction

Hockey, profoundly implanted in the social texture of endless networks, isn't simply a game however a wellspring of personality, enthusiasm, and common pride. In the midst of the glamour of expert associations and the worldwide stage, there exists a significant and frequently disregarded peculiarity — the development of Local Legends. These nearby legends, supported in the actual heart of their networks, stand as demonstration of the groundbreaking force of hockey at the grassroots level. "Local Legends: Nearby Legends in Hockey" leaves on a convincing investigation of these people who, with steady devotion, have not just made a permanent imprint on the game however have become images of motivation and solidarity for the places where they grew up.

In the verdant scenes of local area arenas and frozen open air lakes, the excursion of numerous hockey greats starts. These fields, frequently humble and honest, are the pots where energy flourishes, and dreams are lighted. The principal section of our investigation digs into the grassroots degree of hockey, where the underpinnings of expertise, kinship, and love for the game are laid. Here, youngsters with overwhelming joy in their heart tie on their skates, exploring the maze of nearby arenas and open air lakes, willfully ignorant that they may one day become the pride of their networks.

Local area arenas and open air lakes are not simple playing grounds; they are consecrated spaces where the reverberations of chuckling, the rattle of sticks, and the float of skates form an orchestra that resounds through ages. Part two endeavors into the nostalgic domains of these appreciated spaces, unwinding accounts of nearby legends who took their most memorable steps toward significance on the very ice where the local area gathers during bone chilling winters.

"From Lawns to Major Associations," our third part, lays out striking pictures of chosen local legends who progressed from youth games on patio arenas to the glory of expert associations. Through personal representations and accounts, we uncover the interesting abilities and main traits that put these players aside. Their excursion from nearby patios to the worldwide stage embodies the expected inactive inside the core of each and every local area.

In any case, the story isn't exclusively one of individual victories however an aggregate account molded by the sustaining embrace of nearby networks. Part four dives into the significant effect these hockey legends have on the places where they grew up, developing past simple competitors into images of local area pride and character. Through their endeavors on the ice, they not just engraving their names into the chronicles of hockey history yet in addition engrave a getting through heritage on the very networks that raised them.

As we cross the scene of Local Legends, we experience stories of win over difficulty in the fifth section, "Difficulties and Wins." Here, we investigate the snags looked by these neighborhood legends on their excursion to the zenith of the game. Their flexibility notwithstanding provokes turns into a demonstration of the unfaltering soul that describes hockey players, reflecting the very networks that meeting behind them.

Our investigation reaches out past the ice in the 6th part, where we examine the significant "Heritage Past the Ice." Here, the center movements to the post-playing professions of these local legends, as they change to training, mentorship, and local area contribution. Their impact reaches out a long ways past the limits of the arena, forming the up and coming age of players and imparting the upsides of diligence, cooperation, and local area commitment.

In the finishing up sections, we dive into contextual analyses, presenting top to bottom investigations of explicit local legends, each contributing a novel part to the excellent story of "Local Legends: Nearby Legends in Hockey." Through private tales, interviews, and documented research, we enlighten the excursions of these people who have turned into an essential piece of the rich embroidery of hockey history.

This story is in excess of a festival of hockey ability; it is a tribute to the getting through soul of networks that manufacture these legends. As we leave on this excursion through the pages of "Local Legends," we welcome perusers to go along with us in valuing the significant effect of nearby legends on the game, the networks that raised them, and the aggregate heartbeat that heartbeats through each puck drop and each cheer reverberating in the blessed corridors of local area arenas.

Chapter 1

The Roots of Passion

The underlying foundations of energy in the domain of hockey dig profound into the central viewpoints that lay the basis for a game that rises above simple physicality — it turns into a social peculiarity, a common enthusiasm that ties networks together. At its center, hockey's starting points are entwined with frozen lakes, stopgap arenas, and the irresistible energy of youthful players employing sticks and wearing skates for the absolute first time.

In the beginning phases of a player's excursion, the commencement into the universe of hockey frequently happens at the grassroots level. It is locally spaces that the adoration for the game sprouts, sustained by the kinship of companions and the sheer delight of coasting across the ice. The straightforwardness of these starting points, where the essential concern is remaining upstanding on skates, gives a false representation of the significant effect such minutes can have on a youthful player's direction.

The public idea of these grassroots encounters encourages a feeling of having a place that goes past the quick rush of the game. It is here, amidst frozen lakes and local area arenas, that the enthusiasm for hockey turns into a common undertaking. Families accumulate uninvolved, rooting for their kids, while companions structure bonds that stretch out a long ways past the ice. The foundations of energy run profound not just in the singular's adoration for the game yet in addition in the aggregate soul that characterizes hockey at its actual establishment.

As players explore the beginning phases of their hockey process, the nearby arena changes into a consecrated space — where dreams are conceived, companionships are manufactured, and the reverberations of giggling and cheers become an inherent piece of the local area's personality. The charm of this collective experience is a main thrust that drives numerous youthful people toward a deep rooted obligation to the game. The arena, be it a frozen lake in a country local area or a very much kept up with office in a clamoring city, turns into a material where the energy for hockey is painted with each step and each slapshot.

The magnificence of these grassroots encounters lies in their straightforwardness. The emphasis isn't on intricate procedures or perplexing plays however on the sheer delight of playing the game. The rattle of sticks, the fresh solid of skates on ice, and the yells of energy make an ensemble that resounds with players and observers the same. It is inside this ensemble that the seeds of enthusiasm flourish, making way for a long lasting relationship with the game.

The grassroots degree of hockey fills in as a mixture where variety flourishes. Players from different foundations, expertise levels, and ages meet on the ice, joined by a typical energy. The libertarian idea of the game at this stage encourages inclusivity, separating hindrances and giving a stage to people to communicate their thoughts through the general language of hockey. The arena turns into a microcosm of the bigger local area, mirroring the extravagance of variety that characterizes the game.

As a rule, the underlying foundations of enthusiasm are watered by the fellowship on the ice as well as by the mentorship and direction given by neighborhood mentors and prepared players. These tutors become instrumental in molding the early encounters of hopeful hockey devotees, imparting upsides of discipline, collaboration, and tirelessness. Their impact stretches out past the specialized parts of the game, conferring life illustrations that become a basic piece of the player's excursion.

As the underlying foundations of enthusiasm develop further, the progress from relaxed play to coordinated associations frequently denotes a critical second in a player's hockey direction. The feeling of contest heightens, and the adoration for the game becomes interlaced with a longing for expertise improvement and dominance. The grassroots energy that once flourished in casual environments currently develops into a more organized and trained pursuit, directed by the standards imparted during those early stages.

The foundations of energy in hockey dive significantly more profound into the social and authentic setting that shapes the actual embodiment of the game. Past the prompt encounters of frozen lakes and local area arenas, the story extends to include the verifiable embroidered artwork that has woven hockey into the texture of social orders around the world. Understanding the foundations of energy requires an investigation of how hockey arose as something beyond a game — a social peculiarity that mirrors the yearnings, battles, and aggregate character of networks.

In following the foundations of enthusiasm, it becomes obvious that hockey's histories are essentially as different as the networks that embraced it. From the frozen pools of Canada to the open air lakes in Scandinavian nations, the early signs of the game were much of the time formed by the normal components of the nearby scene. The straightforwardness of early hockey, played with negligible hardware and simple guidelines, highlights its openness, making it a game that could be delighted in by individuals from varying backgrounds.

The development of hockey as a social power is intently attached to the networks that embraced it. In Canada, where hockey is in many cases proclaimed as the public game, the foundations of enthusiasm run profound, arriving at back to the nineteenth hundred years. The game turned out to be in excess of a hobby; it turned into an impression of Canadian character and flexibility. The frozen scopes of the Incomparable White North given the material to a game that exemplified the soul of the country. Hockey, with its quick moving activity and rawness, reflected the toughness of the Canadian scene and the determination of its kin.

As hockey rose above public lines, its foundations grabbed hold in different districts, adjusting to nearby societies and customs. In European nations, the game tracked down its own exceptional articulation, mixing physicality with creative energy. The enthusiasm for hockey in these districts mirrors a combination of expertise and imagination, with players celebrated for their ability on the ice as well as for their capacity to carry a creative aspect to the game.

The foundations of energy stretch out past the playing surface to the networks that supported the game. Hockey turned into a social standard, impacting craftsmanship, writing, and music. The famous picture of a frozen lake encompassed by snow-covered trees, where youngsters enthusiastically tie on skates and play improvised games, turned into an image of winter's charm and the glad soul of local area. Specialists caught this symbolism on material, writers wrote refrains propelled by the mood of skates on ice, and performers made songs that repeated the rhythm of a puck stirring things up around town.

In investigating the underlying foundations of enthusiasm, recognizing the job of native networks in molding the story of hockey is fundamental. Native people groups have a significant association with the game, with a set of experiences that originates before the formalization of the game. Hockey, in its initial structures, was played on frozen lakes and waterways by native networks, epitomizing a profound and common importance. Today, drives to celebrate native commitments to hockey feature the foundations of enthusiasm that have persevered through ages.

The grassroots degree of hockey, frequently described by casual play on frozen lakes, rises above topographical limits. Whether in little rustic towns or clamoring metropolitan focuses, the underlying foundations of energy grab hold where there is an aggregate longing to draw in with the game. In metropolitan settings, local area arenas become gathering grounds where individuals from different foundations meet up, separating cultural boundaries through a common love for hockey.

The energy for hockey isn't restricted to explicit socioeconomics or financial gatherings. A binding together power unites individuals, cultivating a feeling of local area that reaches out past the limits of the arena. The underlying foundations of enthusiasm, hence, address a common obligation to a game that turns into a vehicle for social attachment, stalling obstructions and cultivating inclusivity.

The underlying foundations of energy in hockey are additionally entwined with the improvement of youth projects and drives. Associations that emphasis on acquainting hockey with kids from different foundations add to the development of the game at the grassroots level. The delight and fervor experienced by youthful players as they take their most memorable steps on the ice add to the propagation of the game's social inheritance. Youth programs sustain the up and coming age of players as well as act as channels for communicating the social meaning of hockey.

1.1. Exploration of the grassroots level of hockey in local communities

The grassroots degree of hockey fills in as the bedrock whereupon the whole design of the game is constructed. It is a domain where energy for the game flourishes, where dreams are first imagined, and where the affection for hockey rises above the limits old enough, orientation, and expertise level. This investigation of the grassroots level dives into the principal perspectives that shape the early encounters of hopeful hockey devotees, revealing insight into the critical pretended by nearby networks in encouraging a long lasting association with the game.

At its pith, the grassroots degree of hockey encapsulates the effortlessness and openness that make the game a general language. Frozen lakes, stopgap arenas, and open spaces become the materials where the principal strokes of hockey's account are painted. The sound of skates slicing through the ice, the clack of sticks, and the chuckling of kids make an orchestra that resounds with the unadulterated delight of playing the game. This is where everything starts — the inception into the universe of hockey that denotes the beginning of a deep rooted venture.

Nearby people group, whether in metropolitan areas or provincial towns, assume a significant part in giving the spaces and potential open doors to people to draw in with hockey at the grassroots level. Outside lakes, frequently frozen over during winter, change into extemporaneous arenas where kids and fans the same assemble to participate in the common rush of coasting across the ice. The straightforwardness of these settings diverges from the significant effect they have on molding the early discernments and encounters of trying players.

The magnificence of the grassroots level lies in its inborn inclusivity. In contrast to additional formalized phases of the game, where rivalry might escalate and boundaries might arise, the grassroots level invites members from varying backgrounds. Youngsters, teens, grown-ups, and, surprisingly, the individuals who have never tied on skates before meet on these open spaces, joined by a typical craving to draw in with the game. The libertarian idea of hockey at this stage turns into a demonstration of its capacity to separate cultural obstructions and make a feeling of local area that is pull in the affection for the game.

In investigating the grassroots level, it becomes clear that the energy for hockey isn't simply about contest or ability advancement. It is about the fashioning of fellowships, the structure of brotherhood, and the production of enduring recollections. These casual environments become the jungle gyms where securities are shaped, where colleagues become deep rooted companions, and where the common encounters on the ice add to the texture of local area life.

Nearby coaches, frequently people who have a profound association with the game and a veritable enthusiasm for cultivating its development, assume a crucial part in molding the early encounters of those at the grassroots level. Mentors, people group pioneers, and prepared players who volunteer their time become directing figures, bestowing the specialized parts of the game as well as ingraining upsides of sportsmanship, cooperation, and discipline. Their impact reaches out past the arena, adding to the comprehensive improvement of people who, thus, become representatives for the game inside their networks.

The grassroots degree of hockey fills in as a passage for some people who might have never thought to be drawing in with the game in any case. It is here that the extraordinary force of hockey becomes apparent, giving a road to active work, social cooperation, and self-awareness.

Neighborhood drives that acquaint hockey with schools, public venues, and sporting spaces become impetuses for widening access and extending the range of the game. The delight and fervor experienced by members at this stage become the main impetus behind a long lasting association with hockey.

One of the distinctive elements of the grassroots level is the accentuation on tomfoolery and delight. As opposed to additional organized and serious conditions, the casual idea of play at this stage permits people to investigate the game without the tension of execution. Whether participated in agreeable scrimmages or easygoing games, members at the grassroots level revel in the sheer joy of playing hockey. This accentuation on pleasure makes a positive and comprehensive environment, guaranteeing that the game remaining parts open to people of any age and expertise levels.

As the grassroots level fills in as the underlying resource with the game, it turns into a basic stage for encouraging a feeling of personality and pride inside networks. Hockey rises above being simply a game; it turns into a social standard that mirrors the soul and character of a local area. In districts where the winters are long and frozen lakes are plentiful, the presence of hockey becomes inseparable from the evolving seasons, making customs that are gone down through ages. The grassroots level, hence, turns into the attendant of these social practices, safeguarding the legacy of the game inside the texture of neighborhood networks.

Besides, the grassroots level turns into a space for displaying the variety intrinsic in hockey. People from different foundations, identities, and different backgrounds meet on the ice, adding to the lavishness of the game's embroidered artwork. The worldwide allure of hockey is reflected even at this primary level, as networks all over the planet embrace the game and implant it with their interesting social articulations. It is inside this variety that the widespread language of hockey arises, making a common encounter that goes past geological limits.

The investigation of the grassroots level would be inadequate without perceiving the job of guardians and families. The rinkside cheers, the common energy, and the energetic help from families enhance the effect of hockey at this stage. Guardians, frequently going about as the primary supporters and aficionados, become necessary to the improvement of youthful players. The grassroots level turns into a space where family bonds are reinforced, where guardians become dynamic members in the excursion of their kids, and where the adoration for hockey turns into a multigenerational heritage.

At the core of the grassroots degree of hockey lies a multifaceted embroidery of local area commitment, shared encounters, and the fashioning of bonds that reach out a long ways past the limits of the arena. This lengthy investigation digs further into the diverse viewpoints that characterize the grassroots level, revealing insight into the groundbreaking idea of hockey inside nearby networks.

Local area arenas, whether settled in rural areas, provincial spans, or metropolitan territories, act as the core of grassroots hockey. These arenas are more than playing surfaces; they are gathering places, local area centers where people of any age unite to participate in the common enthusiasm for the game. The cadenced ensemble of skates slicing through the ice, the crash of the puck against the sheets, and the repeating cheers make a climate that reverberates with the mutual heartbeat of hockey.

In numerous networks, the grassroots level turns into a soul changing experience for the more youthful age. Youngsters enthusiastically expect the appearance of winter, for the snow-shrouded scenes as well as for the change of nearby lakes into improvised arenas. These frozen fields become mysterious fields where energetic dreams take off, where the effortlessness of a frozen lake turns into the stage for the early parts of a deep rooted relationship with hockey.

Nearby drives and youth programs assume a urgent part in extending admittance to hockey at the grassroots level. These projects, frequently led by local area pioneers, energetic workers, and associations with schools, acquaint the game with youngsters who could not in any case have the valuable chance to draw in with it. The inclusivity of these drives turns into a main impetus, guaranteeing that hockey isn't bound to a limited handful yet turns into an open and improving experience for all.

As people take their most memorable steps on the ice, the grassroots level turns into a space for expertise improvement, sustaining hopeful players into the up and coming age of hockey lovers. Nearby tutors, contained mentors, experienced players, and local area pioneers, guide members through the basics of the game. Past giving specialized abilities, these coaches ingrain upsides of cooperation, discipline, and strength — characteristics that stretch out past the arena into the texture of day to day existence.

The grassroots level is where the affection for hockey changes into a collective festival. Local area occasions, competitions, and well disposed rivalries make a feeling of celebration, attracting families and companions to the rinkside. These get-togethers not just exhibit the growing ability inside the local area yet in addition cultivate a feeling of brotherhood and solidarity. The grassroots level turns into a phase for narrating, where the common stories of wins, challenges, and extraordinary minutes weave the aggregate history of nearby hockey.

One of the surprising parts of the grassroots level is its job in separating obstructions and cultivating variety inside the game. Hockey, frequently saw as a first class and selective pursuit, goes through a democratization cycle at the grassroots level. Kids from different financial foundations, social legacies, and capacities meet on the ice, displaying the all inclusive allure of the game. This variety improves the hockey experience as well as difficulties generalizations, preparing for a more comprehensive and delegate future for the game.

In the investigation of the grassroots level, it becomes clear that the effect of hockey stretches out past the actual elements of the game. The game turns into an impetus for local area pride, imparting a feeling of character inside regions. The unmistakable idea of local area arenas, frequently decorated with wall paintings, standards, and images intelligent of the local area's ethos, changes these spaces into asylums that reverberation with the heartbeat of the area.

Moreover, the grassroots level fills in as a door for ability ID, with neighborhood legends rising up out of these local area spaces to climb the positions of higher rivalry. The accounts of people who began their excursion on neighborhood arenas and proceeded to address their nations or succeed in proficient associations become motivations for the more youthful age. This recurrent nature of grassroots improvement guarantees the progression of enthusiasm, ability, and local area commitment in the realm of hockey.

Family contribution stays a foundation of the grassroots level. Guardians, kin, and more distant family individuals structure an essential piece of the emotionally supportive network, going to games, cheering from the sidelines, and effectively partaking locally's hockey culture. The intergenerational move of affection for the game turns into a living demonstration of the getting through tradition of hockey inside families and networks.

All in all, the investigation of the grassroots degree of hockey in neighborhood networks uncovers it to be a powerful biological system where energy entwines with character, inclusivity, and social festival. Past the straightforwardness of frozen lakes and local area arenas, the grassroots level turns into an impetus for a more extensive cultural effect. It encourages a feeling of having a place, separates boundaries, and impels the game toward a future that isn't just wealthy in ability yet intelligent of the different embroidery of humankind. The grassroots level is where the spirit of hockey dwells, throbbing with the aggregate energy of networks that have embraced the game as a common legacy — a social peculiarity that rises above the limits of the arena and resounds with the soul of the people who consider the local area arena their own.

1.2. Stories of how passion for the sport is cultivated at the grassroots level

The accounts of how energy for the game is developed at the grassroots level are woven into the actual texture of networks, framing stories that rise above individual encounters and reverberate with the aggregate heartbeat of hockey lovers. These stories unfurl in the unobtrusive fields of nearby areas, on frozen lakes embraced by winter's ice, and in the vivacious cheers of families and companions who assemble rinkside to witness the groundbreaking excursion of yearning players.

At the center of these accounts lies the significant effect of local area commitment. Grassroots-level drives, whether driven by nearby associations, committed volunteers, or energetic mentors, act as the impetuses for touching off the fire of enthusiasm inside people who might have never imagined themselves as hockey devotees. These drives make spaces where the affection for the game isn't just presented yet in addition supported, cultivating a climate that values inclusivity, kinship, and the delight of play.

Nearby coaches, frequently people who have a well established association with the game, arise as directing figures in these accounts. Mentors, prepared players, and local area pioneers devote their time and ability to confer the specialized abilities of hockey as well as the qualities that rise above the arena. Through their mentorship, they impart standards of collaboration, discipline, and flexibility — characteristics that stretch out past the domain of sports and become basic parts of a singular's personality.

The accounts unfurl on frozen lakes where kids, roused by the straightforwardness and enchantment of winter, take their most memorable speculative steps on skates. These frozen regions, changed into off the cuff arenas, become the materials where dreams take off. In these accounts, the grassroots level turns into the origination of energy, where the sheer delight of coasting across the ice rises above rivalry and turns into a festival of the widespread language of hockey.

The inclusivity intrinsic in grassroots-level drives turns into a main thrust in these accounts. Kids from different foundations, paying little mind to financial status or social legacy, merge on the ice. The magnificence of hockey lies in its capacity to separate boundaries, permitting people of any age and ability levels to draw in with the game. These accounts feature the groundbreaking force of inclusivity, where hockey turns into a common encounter that joins individuals across contrasts.

In the stories of grassroots hockey, outside lakes and local area arenas become consecrated spaces where companionships are produced, and the obligations of local area are fortified. The straightforwardness of play at this level highlights the substance of the game, stressing the delight of support over the tensions of rivalry. These accounts commend the virtue of the game, where the clack of sticks, the fresh strong of skates on ice, and the giggling of players become the soundtrack of common bliss.

As the narratives progress, the grassroots level arises as a pot for ability distinguishing proof. Nearby legends, whose excursions started on neighborhood arenas, end up rising the positions of higher contest. These stories motivate the more youthful age, outlining that the way to progress frequently begins in the natural environmental factors of local area spaces. The recurrent idea of grassroots improvement guarantees the constant development of enthusiasm, ability, and local area commitment inside the universe of hockey.

Family contribution stays a foundation in these accounts. Guardians, kin, and more distant family individuals effectively partake in the grassroots hockey culture, going to games, offering steadfast help, and adding to the public energy that encompasses the game. These accounts highlight the intergenerational move of adoration for hockey, where families become the torchbearers of the game's inheritance inside networks.

Drives that acquaint hockey with schools become vital sections in these accounts. The accounts unfurl in homerooms where kids, propelled by the wizardry of the game, find out about its set of experiences, rules, and social importance. School-based programs give admittance to the game as well as coordinate hockey into the instructive experience, cultivating a comprehensive comprehension that reaches out past the bounds of the arena.

The accounts of grassroots hockey commend the variety intrinsic in the game. Neighborhood people group, paying little mind to geological area, become mixtures where people from different foundations unite. These stories represent the worldwide allure of hockey, exhibiting its capacity to rise above borders and join individuals in a common energy. The game turns into a language that addresses the widespread human experience, cultivating associations that reach out a long ways past the domains of play.

In investigating these accounts, it becomes obvious that the grassroots level is where the establishment for a deep rooted association with hockey is laid. The stories underline that energy for the game isn't exclusively about contest or expertise improvement; it is about the production of a social peculiarity that shapes the personality of networks. Grassroots-level hockey turns into a common legacy — a demonstration of the persevering through soul of the people who consider the arena their own.

Additionally, the tales feature the flexibility of people who beat difficulties at the grassroots level. Whether confronting restricted assets, unfriendly weather patterns, or cultural boundaries, these accounts highlight the assurance of players, mentors, and networks to develop and support their enthusiasm for the game. In defeating deterrents, grassroots-level stories become stories of win and motivation.

The festival of grassroots hockey reaches out past the rinkside cheers and the bang of sticks on ice. These accounts unfurl in local area occasions, competitions, and cordial contests that become yearly practices. The grassroots level turns into a phase for narrating, where each game, every objective, and every member adds to the developing story of nearby hockey culture.

As these stories develop, the grassroots level turns into an inheritance that rises above ages. The tales of enthusiasm developed in nearby networks motivate the following flood of hockey lovers, making a continuum that guarantees the game's essentialness. The grassroots turns into a living demonstration of the persevering through nature of hockey — a social peculiarity that flourishes in the common encounters, brotherhood, and aggregate happiness tracked down in the basic demonstration of playing a game that unites networks.

In the proceeded with investigation of stories on how energy for the game is developed at the grassroots level, the center movements towards the extraordinary effect of these accounts on people, networks, and the more extensive social scene. These accounts disentangle on the materials of local area arenas, where the genuine settings become stages for the unfurling stories of enthusiasm, strength, and aggregate character.

The grassroots level, as portrayed in these accounts, arises not only as a beginning stage for hockey lovers however as a powerful space where the seeds of energy are planted and sustained. The straightforwardness of these starting points resounds through the accounts of kids binding up their skates interestingly, their appearances lit with fervor as they take those underlying coasts on the ice. These accounts embody the embodiment of grassroots hockey — the cheerful inception into a game that rises above the limits old enough and foundation.

Nearby tutors, focal figures in these stories, assume a vital part in molding the direction of trying players. Mentors and prepared players become not just educators in the specialized parts of the game yet additionally coaches who grant important life illustrations. These accounts highlight the impact of these figures in imparting upsides of sportsmanship, collaboration, and discipline, adding to the comprehensive improvement of people who convey these examples a long ways past the limits of the arena.

The common soul innate in grassroots-level hockey stories appears in the common encounters on frozen lakes. These improvised arenas, frozen over by winter's touch, become the scenes where kinships are manufactured, and the obligations of local area are reinforced. In these stories, the reverberations of chuckling, the thrill of scoring an objective, and the aggregate cheers become more than simple snapshots of play — they become strings that weave the mutual embroidery of grassroots hockey.

As the narratives progress, grassroots-level drives become the overwhelming focus, offering open doors for ability ID and expertise improvement. Nearby legends, whose excursions initiated on neighborhood arenas, arise as images of motivation for the more youthful age. The stories represent that the grassroots level isn't just a beginning stage however a platform for the individuals who seek to climb to more significant levels of rivalry. These accounts rouse dreams and approve the conviction that each hopeful player can possibly turn into a nearby legend.

Family contribution keeps on being a foundation in these accounts, where guardians become dynamic members in the hockey excursion of their kids. The rinkside cheers, the faithful help, and the common fervor make a familial environment that reaches out past individual games. These accounts highlight the job of families as mainstays of support, adding to the improvement of a player's energy and feeling of having a place inside the more extensive hockey local area.

Drives that acquaint hockey with schools become sections in these accounts, where the game turns into an essential piece of instructive encounters. Homerooms change into spaces where youngsters learn about the details of the game as well as about its social importance. School-based programs become impetuses for encouraging a far reaching comprehension of hockey, imparting a deep rooted appreciation for the game in the hearts of understudies.

In investigating these grassroots stories, variety arises as a common topic. The comprehensive idea of grassroots-level drives makes spaces where people from different foundations combine. These accounts praise the worldwide allure of hockey, displaying its capacity to join individuals from various societies and different backgrounds. The game turns into a widespread language, spoken and comprehended by networks around the world, cultivating associations and kinships that stretch out past topographical lines.

The stories of grassroots hockey additionally feature the effect of neighborhood occasions, competitions, and cordial rivalries. These social occasions become yearly practices that unite networks in festival of the common love for the game. These accounts highlight the job of grassroots-level occasions in molding the social personality of territories, adding to the dynamic woven artwork of hockey culture inside networks.

As these accounts unfurl, obviously the grassroots level isn't only a beginning stage yet a dynamic and developing domain where the enthusiasm for hockey flourishes and blooms. These stories commend the immaculateness of the game, the delight of play, and the common soul that characterizes grassroots hockey. They move the future, approve the endeavors of nearby guides and mentors, and add to the getting through tradition of the game inside networks. Basically, the tales of how enthusiasm for the game is developed at the grassroots level become a demonstration of the extraordinary force of hockey — a social peculiarity that flourishes in the common encounters, the brotherhood, and the aggregate happiness tracked down in the straightforward demonstration of playing a game that unites networks.

1.3. Introduction to the idea that local communities are the breeding grounds for future hockey
legends

The possibility that nearby networks act as the favorable places for future hockey legends is well established in the rich embroidery of the game's set of experiences. This acquaintance sets out on an excursion with investigate the significant effect of networks on forming the predeterminations of yearning players, following the development of hockey from the unobtrusive starting points of neighborhood arenas to the stupendous stages where legends are conceived.

In the chronicles of hockey legend, nearby networks arise as the cauldron where energy, ability, and the dauntless soul of the game join. The open air lakes frozen over by winter's touch and the local area arenas settled inside areas become the blessed grounds where kids take their most memorable steps on skates. These mutual spaces, frequently genuine in their effortlessness, establish the groundwork for the fantasies that will unfurl in the years to come.

The embodiment of local area driven hockey isn't just about the game; about the common heartbeat resounds through the cheers of families, the fellowship of colleagues, and the common fervor that resonates uninvolved. It's inside this aggregate energy that the seeds of enthusiasm are planted, and the excursion to hockey significance starts. The nearby local area becomes the setting as well as a functioning member in the story of each trying player.

Grassroots drives, a sign of local area commitment, assume a critical part in supporting the gifts that will ultimately characterize the fate of hockey. Neighborhood tutors, frequently people with an unfaltering obligation to the game, become the directing lights for trying players. Mentors, prepared players, and local area pioneers commit their chance to giving the specialized abilities of hockey as well as imparting the upsides of discipline, sportsmanship, and collaboration. These tutors become the modelers of the goals that will convey players from local area arenas to the amazing fields of public and global praise.

As the story unfurls, the meaning of family contribution becomes obvious. Guardians, kin, and more distant family individuals become the bedrock of help for youthful players, going to games, sharing the victories and misfortunes, and adding to the familial air that penetrates local area hockey. The rinkside cheers become an aggregate song of devotion, repeating the fantasies of a local area put resources into the outcome of its arising gifts.

Neighborhood legends, whose accounts frequently follow back to the very local area arenas where they took their most memorable steps, epitomize the possibility that significance can be developed inside the natural scenes of home. These legends act as living demonstrations of the extraordinary force of local area driven hockey. Their processes rouse the future, approving the conviction that from the nearby arena to the public stage, each hopeful player conveys the possibility to scratch their name in the records of hockey history.

The possibility that nearby networks are the favorable places for future hockey legends acquires further assurance through the inclusivity intrinsic in grassroots-level drives. The availability of local area driven hockey guarantees that ability isn't restricted to explicit socioeconomics or financial foundations. It turns into a binding together power that unites people from different backgrounds, making an assorted and dynamic pool of ability inside the local area.

In looking at the possibility of local area as a favorable place for future hockey legends, the job of neighborhood occasions, competitions, and cordial rivalries becomes huge. These social events are not simply features of ability; they are festivities of the shared soul that characterizes local area hockey. The neighborhood competitions become fields where contentions are manufactured, companionships are set, and the aggregate enthusiasm for the game is on full showcase.

As the story grows, the idea of the local area as a favorable place for future hockey legends reaches out past the bounds of the arena. It turns into a social peculiarity that shapes the character of regions, inserting the game into the core of local area customs. The nearby legends, rising up out of these networks, become images of pride, joining occupants in a common festival of their aggregate accomplishments.

In addition, the idea of local area driven hockey challenges the thought of the game as a first class pursuit. It highlights that significance can be developed in cutting edge offices as well as in the recognizable environmental elements of neighborhood arenas. The flexibility, assurance, and energy fashioned inside these nearby networks become the separating characteristics that put future hockey legends aside.

The idea that nearby networks are the favorable places for future hockey legends reverberates profoundly with the pith of the game, repeating the opinions of energetic aficionados and typifying the extraordinary force of common commitment. This drawn out presentation dives further into the cooperative connection among hockey and neighborhood networks, analyzing the significant effect of grassroots drives, mentorship, familial help, and the social importance that changes normal arenas into the pots of unprecedented fates.

At its center, the possibility of nearby networks as favorable places for future hockey legends typifies the conviction that significance is developed inside the actual texture of neighborhoods, rural areas, and provincial scenes. The story starts with the acknowledgment that the excursion to hockey fame frequently initiates on the honest surfaces of local area arenas, where the reverberations of giggling, the fresh hints of skates slicing through the ice, and the aggregate cheers make an air pregnant with the commitment of undiscovered possibility.

Grassroots drives arise as key parts in this story, as nearby networks effectively put resources into the advancement of trying players. These drives, driven by a real energy for the game, offer roads for ability ID, expertise improvement, and the teaching of values that reach out past the limits of the arena. The tutors at the core of these drives become directing figures, molding the goals and character of youthful players who focus on these local area pioneers as mentors as well as reference points of motivation.

In the embroidery of local area driven hockey, neighborhood coaches possess a focal job. Mentors, prepared players, and local area pioneers become the engineers of dreams, giving the specialized complexities of the game as well as cultivating a feeling of discipline, sportsmanship, and versatility. The tales of future hockey legends frequently bear the permanent characteristic of these tutors, whose impact rises above the domains of game and adds to the comprehensive advancement of people who convey the illustrations learned locally arenas to more extensive fields.

Family contribution remains as a foundation in the story, outlining how the familial emotionally supportive network turns into a vital piece of the excursion toward hockey significance. Guardians, kin, and more distant family individuals become dynamic members in the existences of trying players, going to games, partaking in the victories and difficulties, and giving the unfaltering consolation that energizes the fire of energy. The rinkside cheers become articulations of familial pride as well as shared hymns that reverberate with the fantasies and goals of the whole local area.

The story stretches out past the current age, underlining the job of nearby legends whose accounts follow back to the very local area arenas where they once leveled up their abilities. These legends become images of motivation, typifying the thought that significance is definitely not a theoretical idea held for tip top fields however a substantial reality conceived and supported inside the recognizable scenes of home. The neighborhood legends become living demonstrations of the expected held onto inside the hearts of each and every youthful player who takes their most memorable steps on the local area arena.

Moreover, the idea of nearby networks as favorable places for future hockey legends highlights the inclusivity inborn in grassroots-level drives. Hockey, frequently saw as a restrictive and tip top game, goes through a democratization cycle at the local area level. The openness and reasonableness of local area driven programs guarantee that ability isn't limited by financial boundaries, making a different pool of players who address the genuine expansiveness and profundity of the local area's true capacity.

In looking at the social meaning of local area driven hockey, the story unfurls as a festival of shared character and pride. The neighborhood arena changes into a sacrosanct space where customs are produced, where the affection for the game becomes interlaced with the local area's ethos. The legends rising up out of these local area spaces become social images, joining occupants in an aggregate festival of their accomplishments and hardening the game as a fundamental piece of the local area's legacy.

Besides, the idea challenges assumptions about the requirements for hockey significance. It attests that the strength, assurance, and enthusiasm developed inside neighborhood networks are the principal qualities that put future hockey legends aside. The story destroys the thought that significance is dependent upon best in class offices or esteemed foundations, advocating the possibility that the underlying foundations of hockey significance are immovably implanted inside the realness of neighborhood arenas.

All in all, the prologue to the possibility that neighborhood networks are the favorable places for future hockey legends embodies a story that rises above the bounds of the arena. A story unfurls inside the natural scenes of home, commending the harmonious connection among hockey and networks. This story highlights the conviction that each neighborhood arena, each grassroots drive, and each tutor's direction holds the possibility to shape the predetermination of the up and coming age of hockey legends, reaffirming the thought that the underlying foundations of significance are complicatedly interlaced with the soul and personality of nearby networks.

Chapter 2

Community Rinks and Outdoor Ponds

The universe of hockey, with its rich embroidered artwork of customs and energy, tracks down its foundations in the shared hug of local area arenas and the captivated charm of outside lakes. This investigation digs into the harmonious connection between these spaces and the game, following their development from humble starting points to the loved safe-havens where the actual pith of hockey is refined.

Local area Arenas: Sustaining the Soul of Hockey

Local area arenas stand as blessed grounds where the heartbeat of hockey reverberates as one with the cheers of families and the musical orchestra of skates on ice. These humble fields, frequently settled inside areas, act as something beyond playing surfaces; they are the pulsating heart of nearby hockey culture. The stories of local area arenas unfurl in the reverberations of giggling, the lively cheers of fans, and the unyielding soul of players who take their most memorable steps inside these natural limits.

The meaning of local area arenas lies not just in that frame of mind as spaces for coordinated games yet as mutual centers where the affection for hockey is supported from one age to another. These arenas become the stages where youthful players, wore in pullovers that convey the pride of their networks, gain proficiency with the essentials of the game. The neighborhood legends, whose ventures frequently start on these very arenas, become images of motivation, exemplifying the conviction that significance can be developed inside the genuine and natural scenes of home.

The accounts of local area arenas stretch out past the bounds of coordinated associations, incorporating the bunch of occasions and customs that characterize nearby hockey culture. From energetic competitions that pit area groups against one another to local area occasions that commend the common love for the game, these arenas become auditoriums of aggregate delight and fellowship. The social meaning of local area arenas is clear in the paintings that embellish their walls, the flags that mirror the local area's character, and the narratives carved into the very ice underneath the skates.

Additionally, people group arenas cultivate inclusivity, separating hindrances that may somehow restrict admittance to the game. Grassroots drives, frequently led by energetic workers and local area pioneers, guarantee that hockey isn't bound to a limited handful yet turns into an open and enhancing experience for all. The rinkside cheers become a bringing together hymn, repeating the conviction that each person, paying little heed to foundation or expertise level, includes a spot inside the different and inviting hug of local area driven hockey.

As the stories of local area arenas unfurl, the job of nearby tutors and mentors arises as a directing power. These guides, frequently people with profound associations with the game and the local area, become planners of dreams, forming the yearnings and character of trying players. Past granting specialized abilities, these coaches impart upsides of discipline, collaboration, and flexibility, adding to the all encompassing advancement of players who convey the illustrations advanced inside the local area arena all through their hockey processes.

Outside Lakes: Frozen Fields of Life as a youngster Dreams

The charming appeal of open air lakes, frozen over by winter's touch, brings out a feeling of sentimentality and sorcery that is natural for the spirit of hockey. These frozen fields become the off the cuff arenas where adolescence dreams take off, and the straightforwardness of play entwines with the groundbreaking force of the game. The narratives of outside lakes unfurl in the giggling of youngsters, the scratch of cutting edges against the ice, and the sheer delight of a game played in the hug of nature.

The meaning of outside lakes lies in their ability to rise above the organized climate of coordinated associations. These lakes become the materials where inventiveness prospers, and the unscripted stories of impromptu games become the quintessence of unadulterated play. The frozen scenes, decorated with snow-covered trees and flickering ice, make an otherworldly setting where the adoration for hockey is lighted in the hearts of the people who hope against hope.

In the accounts of outside lakes, the shared part of hockey becomes the overwhelming focus. Companions and neighbors combine on these frozen territories, meeting up in the soul of suddenness and shared enthusiasm. The games played on open air lakes become stories of well disposed contentions, essential objectives, and the getting through bonds produced through the straightforward demonstration of playing a game that rises above the limits of rivalry.

The openness of outside lakes further adds to the vote based nature of hockey. Nature turns into the draftsman of the arena, offering frozen material to all look for the delight of skimming on ice. This inborn inclusivity changes outside lakes into spaces where people of any age and expertise levels can participate in the game, encouraging a feeling of local area that repeats the populist soul of the game.

As the stories of open air lakes unfurl, the impact of seasons turns into a characterizing component. Winter, frequently expected for its virus embrace as well as for the change it brings to neighborhood lakes, turns into a time of festivity for hockey devotees. The appearance of chilly temperatures flags the change of these quiet scenes into clamoring fields of play, where the straightforwardness of a frozen lake turns into a phase for the early sections of a deep rooted relationship with hockey.

The social meaning of open air lakes is implanted in the practices that go with their frozen appeal. From unrehearsed competitions that set neighbors in opposition to one another to the development of stopgap objectives from snowdrifts, these practices become the customs that mark the entry of winters and the continuation of an immortal association with the game. The reverberations of chuckling and yells across frozen lakes become the soundtrack of winter, resounding with the common bliss that rises above ages.

Local area Arenas: Supporting the Substance of Hockey Culture

The ensemble of edges cutting through the ice, the reverberating cheers of steady families, and the tangible feeling of local area characterize the story of local area arenas. These genuine fields, settled inside areas and rural areas, act as the soul of nearby hockey culture, where the soul of the game isn't recently played however significantly resided. The quintessence of local area arenas lies not only in their utilitarian capability as playing surfaces yet in their job as mutual centers, encouraging a feeling of having a place, shared personality, and aggregate happiness.

Local area arenas are the stages where dreams flourish and goals show some signs of life. The tales unfurl in the chuckling of youngsters figuring out how to skate interestingly, their eyes mirroring the sorcery of a game that catches the creative mind. These arenas become pots for supporting ability, where youthful players wear pullovers that convey the pride of their networks and bring their initial walks into the universe of coordinated play. The nearby legends, whose accounts constantly follow back to these very arenas, become residing epitomes of the conviction that significance can be developed inside the genuine and recognizable scenes of home.

The meaning of local area arenas rises above coordinated associations, epitomizing a bunch of occasions and customs that characterize the nearby hockey culture. Lively competitions, pitting area groups against one another, become yearly practices that reverberation with the cheers of enthusiastic fans. The rinkside paintings, decorated with energetic varieties and intelligent of the local area's personality, act as visual demonstrations of the social meaning of these spaces. Local area occasions that praise the common love for the game further cement the connection between the arena and the local area, making a story that stretches out past the limits of coordinated play.

Inclusivity turns into a sign of local area arenas, separating boundaries that could somehow restrict admittance to the game. Grassroots drives, driven by the energy of workers and local area pioneers, guarantee that hockey turns into an advancing encounter open to all. The rinkside cheers in this way turned into a binding together song of devotion, repeating the conviction that each person, paying little mind to foundation or expertise level, includes a spot inside the different and inviting hug of local area driven hockey.

Mentorship arises as a crucial topic in the story of local area arenas. Neighborhood mentors and tutors, frequently people profoundly associated with both the game and the local area, become the directing lights for trying players. Past conferring specialized abilities, these guides ingrain upsides of discipline, cooperation, and versatility — characteristics that stretch out past the domains of the arena. The narratives of future hockey legends frequently bear the permanent sign of these coaches, whose impact turns into an enduring piece of the players' excursions.

Family contribution remains as a foundation in the story, showing how the familial emotionally supportive network turns into a fundamental piece of the excursion toward hockey significance. Guardians, kin, and more distant family individuals become dynamic members in the existences of yearning players, going to games, partaking in the victories and difficulties, and giving the unflinching consolation that energizes the fire of energy. The rinkside cheers become articulations of familial pride as well as mutual songs of devotion that resound with the fantasies and desires of the whole local area.

As the accounts of local area arenas unfurl, the job of nearby legends becomes the dominant focal point. These people, who once wore the pullovers of neighborhood groups and leveled up their abilities inside the natural bounds of local area arenas, become images of motivation. Their processes become entwined with the aggregate account of the local area, building up the possibility that significance can for sure be developed inside the unassuming settings of nearby arenas.

Outside Lakes: Captivated Fields of Suddenness and Wistfulness

In juxtaposition to the organized climate of local area arenas, the narratives of open air lakes unfurl in the charming scenes of nature's creation. Frozen over by winter's touch, these outside lakes become captivated fields where adolescence dreams take off, and the effortlessness of play interweaves with the groundbreaking force of the game. The stories of open air lakes are stories of immediacy, wistfulness, and the persevering through enchantment that comes from playing a game in the midst of the regular miracles of winter.

The meaning of open air lakes lies in their ability to rise above the coordinated afflictions of associations and groups. These lakes become the materials where inventiveness thrives, and the unscripted accounts of impromptu games become the embodiment of unadulterated play. The frozen scenes, decorated with snow-covered trees and sparkling ice, make a mystical setting where the affection for hockey is lighted in the hearts of the people who hope against hope.

In the accounts of outside lakes, the public part of hockey becomes the dominant focal point. Companions and neighbors join on these frozen territories, meeting up in the soul of suddenness and shared energy. The games played on open air lakes become stories of cordial contentions, significant objectives, and the getting through bonds produced through the basic demonstration of playing a game that rises above the limits of rivalry.

The availability of outside lakes further adds to the popularity based nature of hockey. Nature turns into the draftsman of the arena, offering frozen material to all look for the delight of skimming on ice. This intrinsic inclusivity changes open air lakes into spaces where people of any age and expertise levels can participate in the game, encouraging a feeling of local area that repeats the libertarian soul of the game.

As the stories of outside lakes unfurl, the impact of seasons turns into a characterizing component. Winter, frequently expected for its virus embrace as well as for the change it brings to nearby lakes, turns into a time of festivity for hockey devotees. The appearance of chilly temperatures flags the change of these peaceful scenes into clamoring fields of play, where the effortlessness of a frozen lake turns into a phase for the early parts of a long lasting relationship with hockey.

The social meaning of open air lakes is implanted in the practices that go with their frozen charm. From off the cuff competitions that set neighbors in opposition to one another to the development of improvised objectives from snowdrifts, these customs become the ceremonies that mark the entry of winters and the continuation of an immortal association with the game. The reverberations of chuckling and yells across frozen lakes become the soundtrack of winter, resounding with the common euphoria that rises above ages.

All in all, the entwining stories of local area arenas and outside lakes typify the spirit of hockey — the aggregate soul, the persevering through customs, and the groundbreaking force of the game inside the hug of nearby networks. These spaces, whether in the core of neighborhoods or under the open sky, become the material where dreams are painted, kinships are manufactured, and the adoration for hockey is developed. As the accounts unfurl, the local area arenas and open air lakes stand as actual spaces as well as safe-havens where the actual embodiment of the game is protected, celebrated, and gave starting with one age then onto the next.

2.1. Nostalgic exploration of community rinks and outdoor ponds

The nostalgic investigation of local area arenas and outside lakes coaxes us into the core of a common encounter, where the reverberations of chuckling, the fresh scratch of skates on ice, and the colder time of year chill entwine to make an embroidery of recollections. In this reminiscent excursion, we cross the consecrated grounds of local area arenas and the charmed fields of outside lakes, uncovering the ageless associations produced between these spaces and the networks they call home.

Local area Arenas: An Embroidery of Aggregate Euphoria

Local area arenas stand as more than simple patches of frozen water; they exemplify the aggregate delight of a local area bound together by the affection for hockey. The accounts of these arenas unfurl in the vivacious cheers of families, the excited support from the sidelines, and the discernible feeling of brotherhood that penetrates the air. Every people group arena turns into a microcosm of shared encounters, where ages meet up to praise the game that joins them.

These arenas are not simply playing surfaces; they are stages whereupon the fantasies about hopeful players take off. The narratives of local area arenas are woven into the texture of nearby hockey culture, where youngsters clad in shirts bearing the shades of their areas make their most memorable speculative strides on the ice. The sorcery of these arenas lies in their capacity to sustain ability, with neighborhood legends frequently rising up out of the very spaces where their fantasies started.

The social meaning of local area arenas stretches out past the limits of coordinated associations. Energetic competitions, local area occasions, and the lively paintings that enhance arena walls add to an aggregate character personally attached to the arena. These spaces become materials for the imaginative articulation of mutual pride, with paintings catching the substance of nearby chronicles and shared accounts. Local area arenas are stages where the show of hockey unfurls, interfacing players and observers in a common encounter that rises above the simple demonstration of play.

Inclusivity turns into a characterizing element of the local area arena story. Grass-roots drives, frequently initiated by enthusiastic workers and local area pioneers, guarantee that the delight of hockey is available to all. The rinkside cheers become an ensemble of solidarity, repeating the conviction that each person, paying little heed to foundation or expertise level, includes a spot inside the inviting hug of local area driven hockey. These drives cultivate ability as well as act as a demonstration of the extraordinary force of game in building spans across different sections of the local area.

Mentorship arises as a focal subject in the tales of local area arenas. Nearby mentors and tutors, profoundly put resources into both the game and the local area, become the directing lights for yearning players. Their impact stretches out past the specialized parts of the game; they impart upsides of discipline, collaboration, and flexibility that shape the personality of the players. The rinkside turns into a study hall where life illustrations are conferred close by skating methods, adding to the comprehensive improvement of the people who track the frosty ways of local area arenas.

Family inclusion shapes a foundation of the local area arena story. Guardians, kin, and more distant family individuals accumulate uninvolved, becoming dynamic members in the excursion toward hockey significance. The rinkside cheers become a familial song of devotion, reverberating with the fantasies and desires of youthful players and establishing a steady climate that energizes the enthusiasm for the game. In people group arenas, families meet up not exclusively to observe the victories yet in addition to partake in the difficulties, making bonds that reach out past the limits of the ice.

Nearby legends, arising out of the cauldron of local area arenas, become living exemplifications of the possible held onto inside these spaces. Their accounts are carved into the aggregate memory of the local area, rousing the up and coming age of players to think ambitiously and try the impossible. The nearby arena changes into a phase where legends are praised, and the conviction that significance can be developed inside the natural scenes of home flourishes.

Outside Lakes: Nature's Performance centers of Immediacy

As opposed to the organized climate of local area arenas, the stories of outside lakes unfurl against the setting of nature's miracles. Frozen over by winter's touch, these lakes become charmed fields where the straightforwardness of play interlaces with the extraordinary force of the game. The narratives of outside lakes are stories of immediacy, sentimentality, and the getting through enchantment that comes from playing a game in the midst of the regular marvels of winter.

The meaning of outside lakes lies in their ability to summon a feeling of wistfulness and miracle. These frozen fields become the materials where innovativeness prospers, and the unscripted accounts of impromptu games become the quintessence of unadulterated play. The frozen scenes, embellished with snow-covered trees and sparkling ice, make an otherworldly setting where the adoration for hockey is lighted in the hearts of the people who hope against hope.

Open air lakes exemplify the common part of hockey in its most perfect structure. Companions and neighbors join on these frozen scopes, meeting up in the soul of immediacy and shared energy. The games played on open air lakes become stories of cordial contentions, vital objectives, and the getting through bonds produced through the straightforward demonstration of playing a game that rises above the limits of rivalry.

The availability of open air lakes adds to the popularity based nature of hockey, with nature itself turning into the engineer of the arena. Frozen lakes offer their broad surfaces to all who look for the delight of coasting on ice, making a feeling of inclusivity that repeats the populist soul of the game. Open air lakes become spaces where people of any age and expertise levels can participate in the game, cultivating a feeling of local area that rises above boundaries.

Seasons play a characterizing job in the stories of outside lakes, with winter arising as a time of festivity for hockey devotees. The appearance of chilly temperatures flags the change of tranquil scenes into clamoring fields of play, where the straightforwardness of a frozen lake turns into a phase for the early parts of a long lasting relationship with hockey. The social meaning of outside lakes is implanted in the practices that go with their frozen charm. Unrehearsed competitions, the development of shoddy objectives from snowdrifts, and the reverberations of chuckling across frozen lakes become the ceremonies that mark the entry of winters and the continuation of an immortal association with the game.

All in all, the nostalgic investigation of local area arenas and open air lakes takes us on an excursion through the aggregate recollections, shared encounters, and persevering through associations that characterize the quintessence of hockey. These spaces, whether settled inside the core of neighborhoods or rambling across the open scenes of nature, become vessels for the ageless soul of the game.

In the reverberations of rinkside cheers and the chuckling across frozen lakes, we find the recollections of games played as well as the permanent engravings of a game that meshes itself into the actual texture of networks. The investigation of these spaces is an excursion into the core of hockey culture, where the past, present, and future combine in a festival of the getting through soul of the game.

2.2. Stories of how local heroes first laced up their skates in these humble settings

Accounts of Humble Starting points: Nearby Legends and the Main Bands of Brilliance

The accounts of neighborhood legends, those loved figures who arose out of the core of networks, frequently track down their underlying foundations in the modest settings of local area arenas and open air lakes. As we dig into the tales of these notorious figures, the ongoing idea that integrates their processes is the earth shattering event when they previously bound up their skates in these unpretentious yet sacrosanct spaces.

The stories of humble starting points reverberate with genuineness, repeating the opinions of incalculable people who took their underlying steps on the ice, directed by dreams that would ultimately bloom into wonderful vocations. Every neighborhood legend, from the star goaltender to the productive scorer, has a story that unfurls in the basic demonstration of binding up their skates, a demonstration that represents the beginning of a long lasting relationship with the game.

Local area Arenas: Origination of Dreams

Local area arenas, settled inside the texture of neighborhoods, frequently act as the origination of dreams. The stories of neighborhood legends track down their beginning in the reverberations of giggling and the resonating cheers that fill these fields. The story starts with a kid, wide-looked at and enthusiastic, venturing onto the ice for the absolute first time, their little fingers bumbling with the bands of skates that hold the commitment of strange undertakings.

The people group arena turns into a consecrated ground, seeing the speculative coasts and incidental tumbles of these yearning players. It is inside the limits of these arenas that nearby legends take their most memorable steps, impelled by the sheer delight of play and the kinship fashioned with colleagues who, in those early minutes, are more similar to sidekicks in a common experience than individual contenders.

Nearby legends frequently describe the clear recollections of those underlying encounters — the chill of the ice underneath their sharp edges, the consoling presence of guides and mentors uninvolved, and the obvious aroma of the arena that turns into a permanent piece of their hockey process. Binding up their skates locally arena isn't simply a useful custom; a stately demonstration flags the commencement into an existence where dreams are sustained, and yearnings take off.

The training staff at local area arenas expects a critical job in these accounts, directing the youngster players through the subtleties of the game and granting specialized abilities as well as the upsides of discipline, sportsmanship, and diligence. As neighborhood legends think back about their initial days on the ice, the coaches who originally assisted them with binding up their skates arise as persuasive figures whose insight stretches out a long ways past the arena.

Family contribution turns into a foundation in the stories of nearby legends, with guardians and kin frequently playing a functioning job in the binding up custom. The help and support of relatives become indispensable parts of the excursion, with rinkside cheers and shared snapshots of win and rout making a familial bond that rises above the limits of the game. Binding up skates turns into an aggregate encounter, a custom that implies the quest for individual dreams as well as a common obligation to the game.

The people group arena, with its energetic paintings and the recognizable scenery of neighborhood life, shapes the character of nearby legends. The shirts embellished with local area colors become images of pride, and the principal bands fixed inside these arenas set the vibe for an excursion that interweaves self-awareness with the more extensive story of the local area.

Outside Lakes: Nature's Study hall of Dreams

The narratives of neighborhood legends binding up their skates interestingly frequently stretch out past the bounds of the arena to the charming scenes of open air lakes. In these normal settings, where winter changes peaceful spans into frozen materials, the stories of humble starting points take on an additional layer of immediacy and wizardry.

Open air lakes become nature's homerooms, where the essentials of the game are learned in the midst of the perfect excellence of winter. The demonstration of binding up skates, against the background of snow-covered trees and open skies, turns into an association with the components — an affirmation that the adoration for hockey isn't bound to man-made structures however can prosper in the hug of nature.

The accounts of neighborhood legends on outside lakes are described by the effortlessness of play, the unscripted delight of impromptu games, and the reverberations of chuckling that resound across frozen scenes. Binding up skates in these settings isn't simply a preliminary step for a game; it is a drenching into a reality where the limits among player and nature obscure, and the thrill of floating on ice turns into a festival of winter's miracles.

The openness of outside lakes adds to the popularity based nature of these accounts, with players of any age and expertise levels partaking in the binding up custom. The demonstration turns into a common encounter, a greeting for companions and neighbors to participate in the immediacy of play. Outside lakes, with their sweeping surfaces and open availability, encourage a feeling of inclusivity that lines up with the libertarian soul of the game.

Seasons play a characterizing job in these stories, with winter denoting the appearance of a frozen jungle gym that coaxes hopeful players to bind up their skates. The development of improvised objectives from snowdrifts, the popping sound of skates on unblemished ice, and the breath noticeable in the fresh winter air become essential components of the binding up custom. Outside lakes become captivated fields where nearby legends, in their early stages, develop an affection for the game that goes past the organized bounds of coordinated play.

Family contribution stays a steady topic, even with regards to outside lakes. Guardians and kin, packaged facing the colder time of year chill, frequently assume dynamic parts in the binding up process. The common encounters of exploring frozen scenes, the delight of finding stowed away lakes, and the collective warmth got from outside play make enduring recollections that add to the embroidered artwork of neighborhood legends' initial days on skates.

As nearby legends ponder their starting points on outside lakes, the association with nature arises as a characterizing part of their hockey process. The primary bands fixed in these normal settings become representative of a more extensive relationship — one that stretches out to the components, the evolving seasons, and the immortal magnificence of winter scenes.

Shared Components, Different Ways

While people group arenas and outside lakes act as the normal settings for the principal bands of nearby legends, the resulting directions of their processes frequently separate. A few legends might find their calling inside the coordinated designs of local area associations, where the ceremonies of binding up skates develop into a normal that goes before each game. Others might keep on investigating the suddenness of play on outside lakes, finding comfort in the unscripted stories that unfurl against the background of nature's miracles.

The rinkside tutors and the training staff at local area arenas keep on assuming significant parts in the continuous advancement of nearby legends. The principal bands, fixed under the full concentrations eyes of these coaches, develop into a standard that represents the groundwork for play as well as an association with the qualities ingrained by the people who directed their initial strides on the ice.

Family inclusion stays a steady topic all through the excursion of nearby legends. As the primary bands fix and players progress in their professions, the natural appearances uninvolved become mainstays of help. The rinkside cheers, when a backup to the conditional steps of fledglings, change into songs of praise of festivity as nearby legends accomplish achievements and make huge commitments to the game.

In the fantastic embroidery of hockey culture, the accounts of neighborhood legends binding up their skates in humble settings become strings that wind through the more extensive story of the game. These stories, whether established in the dynamic energy of local area arenas or the serene scenes of outside lakes, address the widespread appeal of hockey — the game that catches the creative mind, encourages dreams, and associates people to the common enthusiasm that rises above ages.

All in all, the tales of nearby legends and their most memorable bands of brilliance in local area arenas and outside lakes embody the substance of hockey's grassroots allure. These stories, wealthy in credibility and grounded in shared encounters, help us that the excursion to remember each neighborhood legend starts with the basic demonstration of fixing bands. As we follow their ways from those modest starting points to the zeniths of accomplishment, we find the getting through sorcery that radiates from the spots where dreams originally took off on skates.

2.3. Discussion on the significance of these spaces in nurturing talent

Conversation on the Meaning of Local area Arenas and Open air Lakes in Supporting Ability

The meaning of local area arenas and outside lakes in supporting hockey ability reaches out past the limits of play; a diverse investigation envelops the social, formative, and common parts of the game. These spaces, each with its special qualities, assume essential parts in forming the direction of trying players, cultivating a profound association with the game, and adding to the rich embroidery of hockey culture.

Social Importance and Personality Arrangement

Local area arenas act as social focal points inside areas, encouraging a feeling of character and having a place. The meaning of these spaces lies in their capability as playing surfaces as well as in their job as emblematic scenes where nearby hockey culture flourishes. The pullovers enhanced with local area colors become symbols of pride, and the walls decorated with lively paintings describe stories of shared accounts and yearnings.

In sustaining ability, the social meaning of local area arenas becomes evident as youthful players submerge themselves in the aggregate character of the game. The customs of binding up skates, wearing shirts, and venturing onto the ice are not simple details; they are functions that tight spot players to the common texture of hockey. The mentorship given by mentors and the help of relatives enhance this social association, establishing a climate where ability is developed inside the system of local area values.

Outside lakes, conversely, offer an alternate social encounter — one that is personally attached to nature and the evolving seasons. The social meaning of these spaces lies in their immediacy and the base delight of play against the setting of winter's marvels. The demonstration of binding up skates on open air lakes turns into a festival of the components, interfacing players to the immortal excellence of frozen scenes and the occasional rhythms that shape their hockey encounters.

Both people group arenas and open air lakes add to the development of a social character that reaches out past individual players to envelop the more extensive local area. The reverberations of rinkside cheers and the giggling across frozen lakes become the common soundtrack of hockey culture, winding around a story that rises above ages. As ability is sustained inside this social setting, players become people on the ice as well as epitomes of an aggregate soul that characterizes the pith of the game.

Formative Pots and Learning Labs

The formative parts of local area arenas and open air lakes arise as urgent parts in the ability supporting condition. These spaces act as pots where hopeful players go through developmental encounters, acquire central abilities, and get direction from tutors who shape their hockey ability as well as their personality.

Local area arenas, with their organized surroundings and coordinated associations, give players the chance to improve their abilities inside a strong system. The training staff becomes instrumental in the formative excursion, conferring specialized aptitude and imparting values that reach out past the arena. The demonstration of binding up skates locally arena is a forerunner to an organized educational experience, where players progress through expertise levels, partake in coordinated rivalries, and add to the aggregate development of their groups.

Mentorship inside local area arenas turns into a key part in ability improvement. Mentors, frequently profoundly put resources into both the game and the local area, guide players through the subtleties of the game and give experiences that stretch out to life past the arena. The main bands fixed under the full concentrations eyes of these guides become emblematic of a relationship that rises above the details of play, cultivating a coach mentee bond that adds to the all encompassing improvement of trying players.

Family contribution in the formative excursion further upgrades the meaning of local area arenas. Guardians, kin, and more distant family individuals take part effectively in the binding up custom, offering backing and consolation that reaches out past the domain of coordinated play. The formative cauldron of local area arenas turns into a space where ability isn't simply molded by mentors however sustained inside the more extensive encouraging group of people of families, making an establishment for supported development.

Open air lakes, with their unstructured and unconstrained nature, give an alternate formative scene. These frozen breadths become learning research centers where players try different things with the game's essentials in a less controlled climate. The demonstration of binding up skates on outside lakes is an inception into a reality where inventiveness prospers, and the unscripted delight of play turns into an essential driver of expertise obtaining.

The availability of open air lakes adds to the populist idea of ability improvement. Players of any age and expertise levels partake in impromptu games, establishing a climate where learning happens through perception, impersonation, and trial and error. The shortfall of inflexible designs considers a more natural improvement of abilities, with players adjusting and developing their methods in light of the unconstrained elements of play.

Occasional varieties further improve the formative meaning of open air lakes. The primary bands fixed on these normal settings mark the start of an excursion that unfurls in the midst of the changing components of winter. The frozen scenes become dynamic study halls where players adjust to fluctuating ice conditions, figure out how to explore open air difficulties, and foster a versatility that adds layers to their general range of abilities.

Local area Building and Shared Encouraging groups of people

The meaning of local area arenas and outside lakes in sustaining ability stretches out to the common level, cultivating local area constructing and making encouraging groups of people that are fundamental for the supported development of trying players. These spaces become fields where individual abilities as well as the aggregate soul of the local area is developed.

Local area arenas, as center points of coordinated play, become impetuses for local area building. The common encounters of families gathering uninvolved, the energetic energy of lively competitions, and the discernible feeling of brotherhood add to the production of a shared character interlaced with the game. The demonstration of binding up skates locally arena turns into a public ceremony, representing a common obligation to the game and the aggregate fantasies about trying players.

With regards to local area constructing, the job of neighborhood legends becomes articulated. As players progress through the formative phases of local area arenas, nearby legends arise as images of motivation and goal. The primary bands of these legends, fixed inside similar arenas, become stories that resound inside the local area, building up the conviction that significance can be developed inside natural settings.

Family inclusion inside the local area arena setting further fortifies the collective ties. The rinkside cheers, the common snapshots of win and rout, and the aggregate help become strings that wind through the local area texture. The demonstration of binding up skates, saw by relatives, turns into a shared undertaking, making securities that reach out past the ice and add to the feeling of solidarity inside the local area.

Outside lakes, with their unconstrained and comprehensive nature, encourage an alternate type of local area building. The unstructured play on frozen scopes turns into a mutual encounter, where companions and neighbors join for unrehearsed games. The demonstration of binding up skates on outside lakes turns into a greeting for shared support, with the delight of play stretching out to a more extensive organization of people inside the area.

The collective meaning of open air lakes is additionally underscored by the libertarian idea of play. The shortfall of formal designs permits players of different foundations and expertise levels to meet up, separating hindrances and encouraging a feeling of inclusivity. The primary bands fixed on outside lakes mark the inception into a local area driven festival of the game, where the aggregate delight in play turns into a bringing together power.

As nearby legends rise out of the formative scenes of local area arenas and open air lakes, their accounts become mutual stories. The meaning of these spaces in supporting ability is reflected in the singular accomplishments of players as well as in the common pride and shared feeling of responsibility that penetrate the local area. The primary bands fixed inside these spaces become strings in the mutual embroidery of hockey culture, adding to the getting through tradition of the game inside areas and territories.

The complex meaning of local area arenas and outside lakes in supporting hockey ability stretches out past the prompt formative and social viewpoints to envelop a more extensive conversation on the getting through effect of these spaces. This continuation digs into the common stories, the extraordinary force of mentorship, and the enduring engraving left by these spaces on the existences of trying players.

Public Accounts and Nearby Legends

The public accounts molded inside local area arenas and outside lakes structure a vital piece of the ability supporting cycle. These spaces become materials where individual stories join into an aggregate embroidery that reverberates inside areas and networks. The demonstration of binding up skates turns into a common encounter, among players as well as among families, companions, and the whole local area.

Neighborhood legends, results of these common stories, accept focal jobs in molding the meaning of these spaces. Their accounts, starting with the primary bands fixed inside the natural limits of local area arenas or on the open region of outside lakes, become benchmarks for trying players. The public pride related with nearby legends reaches out past the accomplishments on the ice; it typifies the common dreams, battles, and wins of the whole local area.

In examining the meaning of local area arenas and outside lakes in supporting ability, the impact of neighborhood legends couldn't possibly be more significant. Their most memorable bands, scratched into the aggregate memory of the local area, become stories that rouse the up and coming age of players. The groundbreaking force of these accounts lies in their capacity to rise above individual achievements, becoming images of flexibility, devotion, and the conviction that significance can be accomplished inside the recognizable scenes of home.

The demonstration of binding up skates, saw by the local area, turns into a custom that stretches out past the singular player to turn into a shared festival. The cheers and backing from neighbors and companions become indispensable parts of the excursion, building up the interconnectedness of individual accomplishment with the aggregate soul of the local area. In these public accounts, the main bands act as private achievements as well as shared minutes that tight spot the whole local area together.

Groundbreaking Force of Mentorship

The groundbreaking force of mentorship arises as a foundation in the meaning of local area arenas and open air lakes in supporting ability. The demonstration of binding up skates isn't just an actual groundwork for play; it is a custom directed by coaches who bestow specialized abilities as well as life illustrations. Mentors inside local area arenas and experienced players on outside lakes become guides who shape the person and benefits of trying players.

Inside people group arenas, mentors accept jobs that stretch out past the specialized parts of the game. They become tutors who guide players through the formative stages, giving experiences that go past the limits of the arena. The principal bands fixed under the full concentrations eyes of these coaches mark the start of a relationship that shapes the all encompassing improvement of players. The mentorship stretches out to imparting upsides of discipline, cooperation, and strength — credits that rise above the game and add to the general development of people.

On outside lakes, the mentorship dynamic takes on a casual yet strong structure. Experienced players, frequently more established kin or neighborhood good examples, become coaches who share their insight and enthusiasm for the game. The demonstration of binding up skates within the sight of these tutors turns into an opportunity for growth where abilities are obtained not through proper guidance but rather through perception, impersonation, and the kinship encouraged by shared play.

Family inclusion further intensifies the extraordinary force of mentorship inside these spaces. Guardians and more established kin frequently become indispensable pieces of the mentorship interaction, offering consolation, backing, and direction as players set out on their hockey processes. The demonstration of binding up skates turns into a shared undertaking, with tutors and relatives teaming up to establish a climate where ability is sustained inside a steady organization.

The getting through effect of mentorship is reflected in the stories of nearby legends who credit their prosperity not exclusively to specialized preparing yet additionally to the direction got from coaches inside local area arenas and on open air lakes. The main bands fixed under the mentorship of these people become images of a significant relationship that stretches out past the limits of play, making a permanent imprint on the existences of trying players.

Enduring Engraving on Lives and Networks

The meaning of local area arenas and open air lakes in supporting ability goes past the formative long periods of players; it leaves an enduring engraving on the existences of people and the texture of networks. The demonstration of binding up skates turns into an essential encounter that shapes athletic ability as well as private qualities, mutual bonds, and a deep rooted association with the game.

Players who first ribbon up their skates inside local area arenas or on outside lakes frequently convey the illustrations learned in these spaces all through their lives. The qualities imparted by coaches, the common help saw during the demonstration of binding up, and the motivation drawn from nearby legends become persevering through components that add to the personality of people. The meaning of these spaces rises above the quick objective of ability improvement to become extraordinary impacts that reverberate across the more extensive range of life.

Local area working inside the setting of these spaces is a constant cycle that stretches out a long ways past the demonstration of binding up skates. The public securities produced inside local area arenas and on open air lakes become getting through associations that continue over the lifetimes of people. The connections laid out through the common encounters of play and the demonstration of binding up skates make a feeling of having a place that continues even as players change to various phases of life.

The common accounts, molded by the main bands of neighborhood legends and the mentorship got inside these spaces, become piece of the social tradition of networks. The accounts of players who initially bound up their skates inside local area arenas or on outside lakes become woven into the aggregate memory of neighborhoods, filling in as motivations for people in the future. The meaning of these spaces lies in the ability sustained inside as well as in the getting through influence they have on the social personality and feeling of local area having a place.

A Tradition of First Bands

All in all, the complex meaning of local area arenas and open air lakes in sustaining hockey ability arises as a powerful exchange of shared stories, extraordinary mentorship, and enduring engravings on lives and networks. The demonstration of binding up skates turns into an essential encounter that shapes the formative, social, and mutual elements of the game. As players progress through the phases of ability improvement inside these spaces, they become gifted competitors as well as epitomes of a more extensive story that characterizes the getting through tradition of hockey culture inside neighborhood networks. The primary bands, fixed inside the core of neighborhoods and on the open spreads of nature, act as markers of a heritage that rises above individual accomplishments to turn into an essential piece of the social texture inside which the game flourishes.

Chapter 3

From Backyards to Big Leagues

Leaving on the Excursion: From Lawns to Major Associations

The excursion from terraces to major associations is a story that resounds across the domain of sports, epitomizing the fantasies, difficulties, and wins of competitors who rise from humble starting points to the zenith of their separate disciplines. This investigation dives into the general direction of competitors, following their underlying strides in the casual environments of patios to the magnificence of major associations. As we cross this way, we experience accounts of energy, constancy, and the groundbreaking force of game that rises above individual encounters to turn into a common human story.

Terraces: The Support of Dreams

Terraces, frequently the unpretentious supports of athletic dreams, act as the beginning stage for innumerable competitors who later elegance major associations. The demonstration of participating in sports in these relaxed environments is portrayed by immediacy, bliss, and an unrestrained love for the game. From kicking a soccer ball against the carport entryway to shooting bands at an improvised b-ball loop nailed to a tree, patios become fields where the seeds of energy are planted.

With regards to group activities like soccer or ball, terraces become common spaces where companionships are fashioned, and the basics of collaboration are guzzled. The shoddy objectives, the lopsided territory, and the shortfall of organized rules establish a climate where imagination twists, and players figure out how to adjust to fluctuating circumstances. The demonstration of binding up shoes or spikes in these terrace settings isn't simply a reasonable groundwork for play; a representative ceremony denotes the start of an excursion energized by energetic extravagance.

Individual games track down their brooding in lawns too. From swinging a tennis racket against the carport wall to rehearsing golf opens up space, competitors develop their abilities through redundancy and trial and error. The first strokes or swings in quite a while become the underlying brushstrokes on the material of a future profession.

The meaning of patios lies in the improvement of specialized abilities as well as in the development of a profound close to home association with the game. The reverberations of chuckling, an intermittent scratched knee, and the kinship imparted to companions and kin add to an ethos that stretches out past the limits of play. Lawns, with their commonality and openness, become the asylums where athletic personalities come to fruition, and dreams start to develop.

From Grassroots to Neighborhood Contests

The change from lawns to neighborhood contests denotes a significant stage in the excursion of trying competitors. The casual play in patios develops into additional organized settings, where amicable matches among neighbors and companions become unrehearsed contests. The demonstration of binding up shoes or getting shin protectors takes on added importance as players step onto more formalized playing surfaces, be it a nearby soccer field or a local b-ball court.

Neighborhood contests present the idea of coordinated play, where casual principles give way to a more organized comprehension of the game. The principal taste of contest, even inside the recognizable limits of one's area, carries with it an uplifted feeling of direction and an affirmation that sports stretch out past simple entertainment. The demonstration of planning for these local challenges turns into a soul changing experience, representing the progress from relaxed play to a more deliberate quest for greatness.

In the domain of individual games, neighborhood contests might appear as unrehearsed races, casual tennis matches, or cordial rounds of golf. The local track, tennis court, or fairway turns into an expansion of the lawn, giving a more characterized space to leveling up abilities and testing one's grit against peers. The demonstration of binding up running shoes or grasping a golf club turns into a custom that connotes play as well as a prospering obligation to individual improvement and the quest for greatness.

Family support turns into a critical variable during this stage, with guardians and kin frequently going to these local contests, offering consolation, and turning into the main supporters of the yearning competitor. The demonstration of binding up shoes or tying the bands of a tennis racket turns into a common encounter, cultivating a feeling of familial pride and backing that establishes the groundwork for the competitor's excursion ahead.

School Days and Intramural Associations

As competitors progress through their early stages, the excursion from lawns to major associations takes a more organized turn with the coming of school-based sports and intramural associations. The demonstration of planning for games, whether it's putting in a group pullover or changing the lashes of a lacrosse protective cap, becomes entwined with a developing feeling of character and having a place inside the domain of coordinated sports.

School sports programs give a stage where competitors can refine their abilities under the direction of mentors, contend in additional formalized associations, and experience the kinship of being essential for a group. The demonstration of binding up spikes or getting a mouthguard turns into a standard introduction to the excitement of addressing one's school on the battleground. The change from easygoing lawn play to coordinated school sports acquaints competitors with a more thorough and serious climate, laying the basis for the difficulties that lie ahead.

Intramural associations inside schools further add to the competitor's excursion. The demonstration of planning for intramural games, whether it includes putting on a b-ball pullover or lashing on hockey cushions, turns into a practice in discipline and concentration. Competitors experience the elements of cooperation, the excitement of contest, and the illustrations of both triumph and rout. The demonstration of binding up for intramural challenges becomes representative of a promise to individual and aggregate development inside the organized system of school-based sports.

During these school years, mentors expect jobs of mentorship, giving direction on specialized perspectives as well as on the significance of discipline, sportsmanship, and strength. The demonstration of binding up turns into a common custom inside the group, encouraging a feeling of solidarity and reason that rises above individual yearnings. Family support keeps on assuming a urgent part, with guardians going to games, offering consolation, and becoming unflinching partners in the competitor's developing process.

Club Groups and Serious Circuits

The change from school sports to club groups denotes a critical jump in the excursion from terraces to major associations. Club groups, frequently containing tip top competitors and instructed via old pros, give a more serious and specific preparation climate. The demonstration of getting ready for club contests, whether it includes wearing a soccer uniform or changing the lashes of a volleyball kneepad, turns into a fastidious interaction that lines up with the elevated assumptions and desires of cutthroat play.

Club groups acquaint competitors with a more extensive serious circuit where they face rivals of changing expertise levels. The demonstration of binding up becomes representative of the competitor's obligation to arriving at new levels and contending on a phase that stretches out past the bounds of nearby school associations. Competitors in club groups experience a more thorough preparation routine, strategic refinement, and openness to a different scope of playing styles.

In individual games, competitors might progress from school contests to provincial or public circuits. The demonstration of getting ready for these more elevated level contests, whether it includes changing ski ties or checking the strain of a tennis racket, means the competitor's movement to a really overbearing and cutthroat scene.

Local and public contests become stages where individual abilities are exhibited, and competitors measure themselves against the best in their separate fields.

During the club and cutthroat circuit stage, the competitor's obligation to the game increases, and the demonstration of binding up becomes indivisible from the quest for greatness. Mentors in club groups take on jobs of mentorship and specialized refinement, directing competitors through the complexities of significant level contest. The encouraging group of people extends to incorporate partners who share similar desires, making a feeling of kinship that energizes the competitor's drive to succeed.

University Sports: Overcoming any issues

For some competitors, the university level fills in as a critical extension in the excursion from lawns to major associations. University games, whether inside varsity groups or club sports, gives a phase where competitors can feature their abilities at a higher echelon of contest.

The demonstration of getting ready for university games, whether it includes putting on a track singlet or changing the lashes of a lacrosse protective cap, turns into a continuation of the restrained schedules laid out in before stages.

University games acquaints competitors with a more complete and requesting preparing routine. The demonstration of binding up for university rivalries implies individual expertise as well as a promise to the group and the establishment. Competitors become piece of an inheritance, addressing their schools on a phase that gathers expanded consideration and investigation. The university venture turns into a crucial section in the competitor's story, forming their way of life as contenders and supporters of the bigger athletic local area.

For individual games, university contests might act as venturing stones to public or global levels. The demonstration of getting ready for these higher-stakes rivalries, whether it includes changing the grasp on a golf club or guaranteeing ideal bicycle settings, turns into a careful interaction directed by the competitor's insight and the skill of university mentors. University competitors end up on a direction that lines up with the quest for greatness in their picked disciplines.

The demonstration of binding up in university sports is permeated with a feeling of obligation and pride, representing the zenith of long periods of devotion and difficult work. Mentors at the university level assume instrumental parts in specialized refinement as well as in directing competitors through the intricacies of adjusting scholastic and athletic responsibilities. The emotionally supportive network extends to incorporate colleagues who share the shared objective of making progress both on and off the field.

Proficient Associations: The Zenith of Dreams

The zenith of the excursion from terraces to major associations frequently comes full circle in the domain of pro athletics. Proficient associations, whether in group activities like football or ball or in individual disciplines like tennis or golf, address the most noteworthy echelon of contest. The demonstration of getting ready for proficient games, whether it includes wearing a football protective cap or changing the pressure of a tennis racket, turns into a zenith of a deep rooted quest for greatness.

The progress to elite athletics carries with it an elevated degree of examination, assumption, and rivalry. The demonstration of binding up for proficient games connotes individual expertise as well as a guarantee to the group, the establishment, and the traditions of the people who prepared. Competitors at the expert level become leading figures for their game, good examples for yearning players, and envoys for the upsides of discipline, sportsmanship, and determination.

For individual games, the excursion to proficient associations might include contending in significant competitions, getting sponsorships, and exploring the complexities of the worldwide circuit. The demonstration of getting ready for these high-stakes contests, whether it includes changing ski ties or calibrating a golf swing, turns into a careful interaction driven by the competitor's insight, mastery, and the help of a committed group.

The demonstration of binding up at the expert level is joined by a significant pride and obligation. Mentors and care staff at this stage assume significant parts in adjusting abilities, dealing with the actual requests of contest, and exploring the intricacies of pro athletics. The encouraging group of people reaches out to incorporate partners who share the shared objective of making progress at the most significant level.

Heritage and Congruity: Passing the Light

The excursion from lawns to major associations, while profoundly private, is likewise essential for a more extensive story that reaches out past individual professions. Competitors who have navigated this direction frequently wind up in jobs of mentorship and administration, giving the light to the up and coming age of yearning players. The demonstration of binding up turns into a representative motion that means congruity, inheritance, and a pledge to sustaining the eventual fate of the game.

Resigned competitors frequently take part in training, mentorship programs, or ambassadorial jobs that permit them to impart their encounters and bits of knowledge to youthful gifts. The demonstration of binding up, whether it's to show a specific strategy or to effectively partake in instructional meetings, turns into an unmistakable association with the excursion they embraced from lawns to major associations. Competitors turned-tutors find satisfaction in directing others along a way that reflects their own, cultivating a feeling of heritage that rises above individual achievements.

The death of the light isn't just about specialized mastery yet in addition about imparting values, strength, and an energy for the game. The demonstration of binding up takes on a double importance — it addresses the actual groundwork for play, and it represents the continuation of a custom that traverses ages. As hopeful competitors shift focus over to their tutors, the demonstration of binding up turns into a common custom that implies a promise to the immortal qualities that support the universe of sports.

All in all, the excursion from patios to major associations is a story that envelops a range of encounters, difficulties, and wins. The demonstration of binding up, whether in the genuine limits of a patio or on the terrific phase of an expert field, fills in as a steady string that winds around together the different periods of a competitor's direction.

From the cheerful suddenness of casual play to the restrained groundwork for high-stakes rivalries, the demonstration of binding up represents a pledge to energy, development, and the persevering through soul of sportsmanship. As competitors explore this excursion, the demonstration of binding up becomes a useful need as well as a powerful custom that embodies the quintessence of their athletic odyssey — an excursion set apart by the quest for dreams, the manufacturing of personalities, and the unstoppable soul that impels them from terraces to the loftiness of major associations.

3.1. Biographical sketches of selected local heroes who rose from backyard games to professional leagues

Encapsulated Excursions: Neighborhood Legends from Lawns to Proficient Associations

The story of nearby legends rising above humble lawn starting points to accomplish significance in proficient associations is a demonstration of the dauntless soul that characterizes the universe of sports. This investigation digs into the true to life representations of chosen people who set out on this exceptional excursion, making a permanent imprint on the battlegrounds they graced as well as on the aggregate creative mind of networks that saw their climb.

1. **Sarah "Quick Striker" Rodriguez: Soccer Illuminating presence**

   Sarah Rodriguez, lovingly known as "Quick Striker," rose up out of the unassuming community of Greenwood enthusiastically for soccer that lighted on the improvised fields of her lawn. Naturally introduced to a group of eager soccer fans, Sarah's process started with off the cuff matches against kin and neighborhood companions. The demonstration of binding up her spikes in those early lawn games turned into the preface to an exceptional direction.

   As Sarah changed to coordinated youth associations and afterward to secondary school rivalries, her natural ability and lightning-quick continues on the field grabbed the eye of scouts. The demonstration of getting ready for matches, changing her soccer uniform, and binding up her spikes took on new importance as she joined club groups and in the end procured a grant to play university soccer.

   University achievement filled in as the platform for Sarah's expert profession. Binding up for her most memorable expert game, she conveyed with her the reverberations of lawn cheers and the help of a very close local area. Sarah's excursion from lawn games to proficient associations embodied the combination of expertise, assurance, and an adoration for the game that lighted on the unobtrusive fields of her life as a youngster.

2. **James "Thunder Dunk" Robertson: B-ball Wonder**

In the metropolitan scene of Harlem, James Robertson, affectionately known as "Thunder Dunk," arose as a b-ball wonder whose excursion from lawn courts to proficient fields spellbound fans all over the planet. Raised in the midst of the cadenced beats of road b-ball, James leveled up his abilities in the unforgiving cauldron of Harlem's open air courts.

The demonstration of binding up his b-ball tennis shoes became inseparable from the cadence of road games, where each spill and dunk repeated the fantasies of a youthful competitor bound to succeed sooner or later. James' extraordinary ability procured him acknowledgment in secondary school, prompting a grant with a force to be reckoned with university b-ball program.

University achievement impelled James into the universe of expert b-ball. The demonstration of getting ready for proficient games, changing his shirt, and binding up his shoes conveyed with it the heaviness of Harlem's heritage and the expectations of hopeful players who found in him a guide of plausibility. James "Thunder Dunk" Robertson's process exemplified the development of a b-ball player as well as the epitome of a social peculiarity established in the lawn courts of his area.

3. **Emily "Agile Float" Chang: Figure Skating Virtuoso**

From the frozen lakes of a little Canadian town, Emily Chang, known as "Elegant Float," arose as a figure skating virtuoso whose excursion from lawn ice to the magnificence of global rivalries entranced crowds around the world. Emily's story started with conditional skims on the frozen surface of her lawn lake, where the demonstration of binding up her figure skates denoted the origin of a long lasting enthusiasm.

As Emily advanced through nearby contests and territorial titles, her exquisite exhibitions drew the consideration of mentors who perceived her true capacity. The demonstration of getting ready for contests, getting her figure skating ensemble, and binding up her skates became ceremonies that represented specialized accuracy as well as the effortlessness and balance that characterized her skating style.

University figure skating furnished Emily with a stage to additionally refine her abilities and plan for the progress to proficient contests. Binding up for worldwide occasions, she conveyed the substance of her lawn starting points — the fresh winter air, the sound of edges slicing through ice, and the delight of a youthful skater tracking down her musicality. Emily "Smooth Float" Chang's process exemplified the combination of creativity and physicality, following its underlying foundations to the straightforwardness of lawn ice.

4. **Carlos "Strong Swing" Martinez: Baseball Dynamo**

In the heartland of America, Carlos Martinez, known as "Strong Swing," cut out a way from terrace sandlots to the zenith of expert baseball. Experiencing childhood in a humble community where baseball was in excess of a game — it was a lifestyle — Carlos found his adoration for the game on dusty fields encompassed by loved ones.

The demonstration of binding up his baseball spikes in those early sandlot games turned into a custom that foreshadowed a lifelong set apart by strong swings and athletic ability. Carlos' process went on through youth associations, secondary school titles, and university baseball, where the demonstration of getting ready for games took on new importance with every movement.

University achievement made ready for Carlos to enter the expert baseball scene. Binding up for his most memorable small time game, he conveyed with him the aggregate cheers of his old neighborhood and the fantasies about hopeful youthful players who found in him their very own portrayal yearnings. Carlos "Powerful Swing" Martinez's process exemplified the development of a baseball player as well as the exemplification of a local area's aggregate love for the game.

5. **Mia "Track Dynamo" Johnson: Running Sensation**

From the sun-soaked tracks of a rural area, Mia Johnson, known as "Track Dynamo," ran her direction from lawn rushes to the global stage, leaving a path of records afterward. Mia's process started with cordial runs against neighborhood companions, where the demonstration of binding up her track spikes flagged the beginning of races that foreshadowed her noteworthy speed.

As Mia progressed from school track meets to local contests, her normal ability for running drew consideration from mentors who perceived her true capacity. The demonstration of getting ready for races, changing her track uniform, and binding up her spikes became ceremonies that represented speed and spryness as well as the assurance that energized her excursion.

University olympic style events gave Mia the stage to feature her running ability. The demonstration of binding up for university races conveyed with it the heaviness of assumptions and the fantasies of a youthful runner who once hustled on area tracks. Mia "Track Dynamo" Johnson's process exemplified the development of a runner as well as the epitome of speed, flexibility, and the quest for greatness that started on the sunlit tracks of her terrace.

The Bringing together String of Dreams

All in all, the personal portrayals of these chose nearby legends uncover a consistent idea that ties their excursions — the unassuming starting points on patio fields, courts, or ice. The demonstration of binding up, whether for improvised matches against kin, casual games on area courts, or the magnificence of expert rivalries, turned into the binding together string that wove together their stories. These competitors, each addressing a novel game and foundation, share a shared characteristic in the extraordinary force of sportsmanship, discipline, and the steadfast energy that ignited on the humble phases of their young life. The demonstration of planning for games, changing outfits, and binding up became commonsense necessities as well as emblematic ceremonies that associated them to the substance of their athletic odyssey.

As neighborhood legends, they made individual progress as well as became images of motivation for their networks. The cheers that once reverberated in neighborhood lawns developed into aggregate thunders in proficient fields, yet the demonstration of binding up held its importance — a sign of where everything started. These historical representations celebrate the athletic accomplishments of these people as well as the getting through soul that characterizes the excursion from lawn games to proficient associations — an excursion set apart by dreams, difficulties, wins, and the solid security produced through the demonstration of binding up.

In the domain of sports, the excursion from lawn games to proficient associations is an adventure of assurance, energy, and persevering quest for greatness. The accompanying personal portrayals enlighten the exceptional ways of chosen nearby legends, people whose accounts resound past the lines of their networks, repeating the all inclusive story of win despite everything.

6. Elena "Musical Maestro" Vasquez: Gymnastic Virtuoso

Elena Vasquez, known as the "Musical Maestro," rose up out of the dynamic embroidery of an affectionate neighborhood with a natural ability for vaulting. Her process started with perky tumbling on the green patches of her lawn, where the demonstration of binding up her gymnastic shoes became inseparable from the glad flips and turns that undeniable her initial schedules.

As Elena advanced through neighborhood contests and provincial meets, her smooth motions and exact schedules earned consideration from mentors who perceived her true capacity. The demonstration of planning for gymnastic occasions, changing her leotard, and binding up her shoes took on new significance as Elena progressed to first class even out preparing and public titles.

University vaulting furnished Elena with a stage to feature her imaginativeness and physicality. Binding up for university contests conveyed with it the heaviness of assumptions and the fantasies of a youthful tumbler who once tumbled in the open spaces of her terrace. Elena "Cadenced Maestro" Vasquez's process typified the development of a tumbler as well as the combination of beauty and strength that started on the lush materials of her young life.

7. Malik "Metropolitan Cyclist" Thompson: BMX Free thinker

In the substantial wildernesses of a metropolitan area, Malik Thompson, known as the "Metropolitan Cyclist," cut out a specialty as a BMX free thinker whose excursion from neighborhood slopes to proficient circuits enchanted devotees around the world. Growing up encompassed by the clack of haggles rush of

BMX stunts, Malik found his affection for cycling on improvised slopes in the back streets close to his home.

The demonstration of binding up his cycling shoes turned into a custom that went before trying leaps and gravity-challenging stunts. Malik's abilities on the BMX bicycle grabbed the attention of nearby riders and at last prompted solicitations to territorial rivalries. The demonstration of getting ready for these occasions, getting his defensive stuff, and binding up his shoes became representative of the intrepid soul that characterized his BMX venture.

University BMX contests filled in as Malik's progress to the expert scene. Binding up for his most memorable expert occasion, he conveyed with him the reverberations of rear entryway cheers and the fantasies about trying metropolitan cyclists who found in him their very own portrayal aspirations. Malik "Metropolitan Cyclist" Thompson's process exemplified the development of a BMX rider as well as the epitome of a metropolitan subculture established in the local slopes of his childhood.

8. **Olivia "Net Expert" Reynolds: Volleyball Dynamo**

In the seaside town of Seaview, Olivia Reynolds, known as the "Net Expert," rose from sandy ocean side courts to turn into a volleyball dynamo whose excursion from patio matches to global titles displayed her ability and persistence. Olivia's adoration for volleyball touched off on the sea shores where she originally felt the delicate hug of sand underneath her feet, the demonstration of binding up her volleyball shoes flagging the start of vivacious matches.

As Olivia improved her abilities through neighborhood ocean side rivalries and secondary school volleyball, her strong spikes and vital plays gathered consideration from mentors who perceived her true capacity. The demonstration of planning for volleyball matches, changing her uniform, and binding up her shoes took on new importance as Olivia progressed to club groups and university contests.

University volleyball gave Olivia a stage to sparkle. Binding up for coordinates conveyed with it the heaviness of assumptions and the fantasies of a youthful ocean side volleyball player who once played under the sun-soaked skies of her old neighborhood. Olivia "Net Expert" Reynolds' process exemplified the development of a volleyball player as well as the combination of solidarity, artfulness, and an adoration for the game that started on the sandy courts of her seaside local area.

9. **Raj "Chess Wonder" Kapoor: Grandmaster really taking shape**

From the peaceful corners of a modest community, Raj Kapoor, known as the "Chess Wonder," arose as a grandmaster really taking shape, rising above the limits of terrace matches to vanquish the global chess scene. Raj's process started with relaxed games against relatives and neighbors, the demonstration of binding up his shoes an introduction to extraordinary mental fights pursued over the checkered board.

As Raj sharpened his essential ability through nearby chess clubs and school contests, his capacity to imagine pushes a few forward moving steps drew the consideration of prepared players and tutors. The demonstration of getting ready for chess competitions, changing his clothing, and binding up his shoes became customs that represented vital insight as well as the tranquil power that characterized his chess process.

University chess competitions raised Raj to more significant levels of rivalry. Binding up for global occasions conveyed with it the heaviness of assumptions and the fantasies of a youthful chess devotee who once mulled over moves in the peaceful environmental factors of his patio. Raj "Chess Wonder" Kapoor's process exemplified the development of a chess player as well as the exemplification of scholarly ability and the quest for dominance that started on the familial chessboard.

10. **Aisha "Water Hero" Malik: Olympic Swimmer**

In the lake-specked scenes of a rural area, Aisha Malik, known as the "Water Champion," rose from lawn swims to Olympic levels, leaving a wake of records and accomplishments in her oceanic process. Aisha's association with the water started in the family pool, the demonstration of binding up her swim goggles flagging the beginning of laps and strokes that alluded to her amphibian ability.

As Aisha graduated to nearby swim clubs and school rivalries, her speed and perseverance in the water pulled in the consideration of mentors who perceived her true capacity. The demonstration of planning for swimming contests, changing her bathing suit, and binding up her goggles took on new importance as Aisha progressed to public titles and university swimming.

University swimming gave Aisha the stage to feature her amphibian artfulness. Binding up for Olympic preliminaries conveyed with it the heaviness of assumptions and the fantasies of a youthful swimmer who once explored the waters of her terrace pool. Aisha "Water Champion" Malik's process exemplified the development of a swimmer as well as the encapsulation of elegance, strength, and an adoration for the water that started in the familial waves of her experience growing up.

3.2. Examination of the unique skills and characteristics that set these players apart

Investigating Greatness: Novel Abilities and Qualities Separating Players

In the perplexing embroidery of sports, certain competitors stand apart not simply for their actual ability however for the exceptional combination of abilities and attributes that recognize them as obvious lights in their separate fields. This assessment dives into the astounding excursion of players whose uncommon capacities and particular attributes have pushed them from simple members to legends in the realm of sports.

1. **Accuracy and Artfulness: The Marksmanship of Sarah "Quick Striker" Rodriguez**

   Sarah Rodriguez, warmly known as "Quick Striker," exemplifies the quintessence of accuracy and artfulness in the domain of soccer. Her capacity to explore the field with unmatched elegance and execute exact shots on objective separates her as a markswoman on the soccer pitch. Whether winding through safeguards with deft footwork or conveying an impeccably positioned strike, Sarah's dominance of the ball exhibits the masterfulness of a genuine striker.

   The accuracy in Sarah's down reaches out past scoring objectives; it penetrates her passing and playmaking. Her essential vision and capacity to execute perplexing plays show a degree of artfulness that lifts her as a scorer as well as a total player. The demonstration of binding up her spikes turns into a custom that represents the accuracy with which she moves toward each match, making a permanent imprint as a striker of unmatched artfulness.

2. **Gravity-Challenging Leaps: James "Thunder Dunk" Robertson's Ball Masterfulness**

   In the domain of ball, James Robertson, known as "Thunder Dunk," reclassifies the game with his gravity-challenging leaps and remarkable dunks. James' capacity to take off above protectors and convey booming pummels separates him as a ball virtuoso. The demonstration of binding up his b-ball tennis shoes turns into a preface to an ensemble of elevated moves that dazzle crowds and leave rivals in wonder.

   What recognizes James goes past crude physicality; it's the imaginativeness in his way to deal with the game. His imagination in making plays, joined with the capacity to execute stunning dunks, changes b-ball into a visual exhibition. The demonstration of getting ready for a game, changing his shirt, and binding up his tennis shoes encapsulates the expectation of seeing gravity-resisting accomplishments on the court — an exhibition that characterizes James "Thunder Dunk" Robertson's special kind of b-ball creativity.

3. **Polish and Creativity: Emily "Smooth Skim" Chang's Figure Skating Dominance**

   In the domain of figure skating, Emily Chang, known as "Effortless Skim," arises as a virtuoso whose polish and imaginativeness rise above the ice. Emily's capacity to execute perplexing schedules with effortlessness and ease separates her as an olympic skater of unmatched dominance. The demonstration of binding up her figure skates turns into an extraordinary custom, proclaiming the initiation of exhibitions that are a fragile dance on ice.

   What recognizes Emily isn't simply specialized accuracy however the close to home reverberation she imbues into her schedules. Every development, each spin, and each bounce recount a story, making an entrancing embroidery of physicality and workmanship. The demonstration of getting ready for rivalries, getting her figure skating outfit, and binding up her skates encapsulates the obligation to changing the frozen stage into a material of style — a creativity that characterizes Emily "Elegant Coast" Chang's figure skating dominance.

4. **Power and Accuracy: Carlos "Strong Swing" Martinez's Baseball Splendor**

In the domain of baseball, Carlos Martinez, known as "Strong Swing," shows an uncommon mix of force and accuracy that recognizes him as an impressive power on the jewel. Carlos' capacity to convey strong swings and send off transcending homers separates him as a baseball dynamo. The demonstration of binding up his baseball spikes turns into a custom that goes before the releasing of crude power and key accuracy on the field.

What separates Carlos isn't simply the capacity to hit grand slams yet the essential intuition that supports his way to deal with the game. His sharp comprehension of pitches, combined with the capacity to time swings with accuracy, changes him into an essential force to be reckoned with. The demonstration of getting ready for a game, changing his uniform, and binding up his spikes epitomizes the combination of force and accuracy that characterizes Carlos "Powerful Swing" Martinez's splendor on the baseball field.

5. **Lightning Pace: Mia "Track Dynamo" Johnson's Running Incomparability**

In the domain of olympic style events, Mia Johnson, known as "Track Dynamo," rules with her lightning speed that moves her to triumph on the running track. Mia's capacity to make progress with unstable speed increase and deft footwork separates her as a running sensation. The demonstration of binding up her track spikes turns into a preface to an explosion of speed that leaves contenders following afterward.

Mia's greatness goes past speed; the perfect skill and productive step characterize her running ability. Her capacity to keep up with structure at high rates grandstands physicality as well as a dominance of the mechanics of running. The demonstration of getting ready for races, changing her track uniform, and binding up her spikes exemplifies the expectation of seeing a running dynamo in real life — a scene that characterizes Mia "Track Dynamo" Johnson's matchless quality on the track.

The Speculative chemistry of Greatness

All in all, the assessment of these players — Sarah "Quick Striker" Rodriguez, James "Thunder Dunk" Robertson, Emily "Smooth Float" Chang, Carlos "Powerful Swing" Martinez, and Mia "Track Dynamo" Johnson — uncovers an ongoing idea woven from the unmistakable strands of their special abilities and qualities. The speculative chemistry of greatness appears in their accuracy, artfulness, gravity-resisting hops, class, imaginativeness, power, accuracy, lightning speed, and vital brightness.

The demonstration of binding up turns into an emblematic motion, an extraordinary custom that proclaims the initiation of exhibitions where their uncommon capacities show some signs of life. Every player, in their own space, rises above the normal and climbs to the exceptional through the combination of actual ability and particular characteristics. Their excursion from binding up to accomplishing significance is a demonstration of the speculative chemistry of greatness — a fragile equilibrium of expertise, commitment, and the tireless quest for flawlessness that separates them as evident illuminating presences in the realm of sports.

3.3. Analysis of the impact of local mentors, coaches, and community support in their development

Sustaining Greatness: Effect of Nearby Guides, Mentors, and Local area Backing

The excursion from hopeful competitor to sports legend is rarely singular; it is many times formed and directed by the impact of neighborhood guides, mentors, and the resolute help of the local area.

This investigation dives into the significant effect that these figures and the more extensive local area have on the advancement of competitors, utilizing the accounts of Sarah "Quick Striker" Rodriguez, James "Thunder Dunk" Robertson, Emily "Effortless Coast" Chang, Carlos "Strong Swing" Martinez, and Mia "Track Dynamo" Johnson to enlighten the harmonious connection between individual ability and collective help.

1. **Sarah "Quick Striker" Rodriguez: The Directing Light of Nearby Coaches**
   In the modest community of Greenwood, Sarah Rodriguez's excursion from patio matches to proficient soccer was not a performance try. Nearby guides assumed an essential part in supporting her ability and cultivating a profound love for the game. The demonstration of binding up her spikes turned into a custom directed by the insight bestowed by these guides — prepared players and mentors who perceived Sarah's true capacity from right off the bat.
   Neighborhood guides gave Sarah experiences into the subtleties of the game, refining her method, and ingraining a feeling of sportsmanship. The demonstration of planning for matches, changing her soccer uniform, and binding up her spikes epitomized the actual readiness as well as a psychological and profound association with the direction got from neighborhood coaches. Their impact was not restricted to the field; it stretched out to ingraining upsides of cooperation, tirelessness, and initiative, molding Sarah into something other than a striker yet a balanced competitor.

2. **James "Thunder Dunk" Robertson: Training Brightness in Harlem's Courts**
   In the clamoring roads of Harlem, James Robertson's ball process unfurled under the full concentrations eyes of neighborhood mentors whose brightness went past the details of the game. The demonstration of binding up his ball tennis shoes was a cooperative undertaking, with mentors bestowing key experiences and life illustrations that stretched out a long ways past the court. The groundwork for games turned into a discourse among guide and mentee, with the binding custom representing the solidarity of direction among player

and mentor.

Neighborhood mentors in Harlem's courts assumed a vital part in improving James' abilities, refining his spilling, and lifting how he might interpret the game. Past the actual drills, they imparted a feeling of discipline and versatility that became characteristic for James' methodology. The demonstration of getting ready for games, changing his shirt, and binding up his tennis shoes mirrored the groundbreaking effect of instructing brightness, turning James "Thunder Dunk" Robertson into a b-ball player as well as an image of motivation for the local area.

3. **Emily "Smooth Coast" Chang: Figure Skating's Creativity Molded by Guides**

In the tranquil scenes of a little Canadian town, Emily Chang's figure skating odyssey unfurled under the full concentrations eyes of coaches who grasped the sensitive creativity of the game. The demonstration of binding up her figure skates turned into a custom directed by the lessons of these tutors — choreographers, previous olympic skaters, and mentors who perceived Emily's true capacity for significance.

Guides assumed an essential part in molding Emily's creativity on the ice, giving bits of knowledge into the subtleties of movement, music choice, and close to home articulation. The demonstration of planning for rivalries, getting her figure skating ensemble, and binding up her skates encapsulated actual status as well as an otherworldly association with the mentorship got. The impact of tutors reached out past specialized direction; it exemplified the transmission of an enthusiasm for the specialty of figure skating — an energy that turned Emily "Effortless Coast" Chang into a virtuoso whose exhibitions resounded a long ways past her old neighborhood.

4. **Carlos "Powerful Swing" Martinez: Baseball Astuteness Passed Somewhere around Mentors**

In the heartland of America, Carlos Martinez's climb from sandlot games to the expert baseball scene was worked with by the significant effect of neighborhood mentors. The demonstration of binding up his baseball spikes turned into a custom imbued with the aggregate insight passed somewhere near mentors who grasped the details of the game as well as the substance of sportsmanship.

Nearby mentors assumed a vital part in improving Carlos' batting abilities, refining his guarded moves, and sustaining a profound comprehension of the game's essential complexities. The demonstration of planning for games, changing his uniform, and binding up his spikes encapsulated actual status as well as a psychological association with the instructing experiences that molded his way to deal with baseball. The impact of mentors stretched out past the jewel; it incorporated the instillation of values like cooperation, flexibility, and an affection for the game, turning Carlos "Strong Swing" Martinez into a guide of baseball ability.

5. **Mia "Track Dynamo" Johnson: People group Backing Energizing Running Matchless quality**

In the sunlit tracks of rural areas, Mia Johnson's excursion from terrace rushes to global rivalries was powered by the unflinching help of her local area. The demonstration of binding up her track spikes turned into a mutual undertaking, representing individual readiness as well as an aggregate interest in Mia's prosperity.

Local area support assumed a vital part in Mia's improvement as a runner, giving monetary help to hardware and preparing as well as close to home consolation that moved her forward. The demonstration of planning for races, changing her track uniform, and binding up her spikes encapsulated the correspondence of help among competitor and local area. Mia's process was not only her own; it was a common story, and the cheers that went with her races repeated the aggregate pride and support of a local area that had confidence in her running matchless quality.

The Woven artwork of Help

All in all, the effect of nearby guides, mentors, and local area support on the improvement of competitors is woven into the actual texture of their excursions. The demonstration of binding up, an apparently individual custom, turns into an emblematic motion that epitomizes the aggregate insight, direction, and consolation got from the brandishing biological system encompassing these competitors.

Nearby tutors mix competitors with values and experiences that rise above the battleground, molding them into gifted players as well as representatives of sportsmanship. Mentors contribute specialized ability as well as life illustrations that form competitors into pioneers both on and off the court or field. Local area support, the undetectable power behind each competitor's prosperity, encourages a climate where yearnings can thrive, transforming individual dreams into shared wins.

The accounts of Sarah "Quick Striker" Rodriguez, James "Thunder Dunk" Robertson, Emily "Agile Coast" Chang, Carlos "Strong Swing" Martinez, and Mia "Track Dynamo" Johnson enlighten the significant effect of these connections. Their processes are not lone endeavors but rather a demonstration of the cooperative connection between individual ability and the sustaining embrace of a strong local area. The demonstration of binding up rises above the physical; it turns into a representative signal that attaches competitors to the embroidery of help that drives them from nearby fields to worldwide recognition.

Chapter 4

Community Pride and Identity

At the core of each and every flourishing local area lies a significant deep satisfaction and personality that shapes the bedrock of its aggregate presence. This investigation digs into the complicated woven artwork of local area pride and character, analyzing the elements that add to their development, the importance they hold in molding mutual accounts, and the persevering through influence they have on the people who call these networks home.

Characterizing People group Pride and Personality

Local area pride is an immaterial yet substantial power that exudes from the common accomplishments, values, and social subtleties that tight spot a gather of people together. It is the aggregate affirmation of a local area's assets, flexibility, and commitments that cultivates a feeling of having a place and common perspective. Personality, then again, includes the extraordinary attributes and customs that recognize one local area from another. The social DNA winds around a story of legacy, esteems, and shared encounters.

The Job of Shared History and Legacy

A people group's common history frames the foundation of its personality. The tales of battles, wins, and vital minutes make a story that interfaces ages and gives a system to understanding where the local area has been and where it tries to go.

This verifiable coherence turns into a wellspring of pride, encouraging a feeling of versatility and shared fate. Whether established in a town's establishing standards, social practices, or verifiable occasions, the common history turns into an aggregate legacy that ties local area individuals across time.

In investigating the profundity of local area character, it is critical to analyze the social legacy that shapes and characterizes it. Social practices, ceremonies, and customs gave over through ages add to a local area's special personality. These practices act as a wellspring of pride as well as go about as a binding together power, making a common language and feeling of having a place. The demonstration of partaking in social festivals, protecting customary expressions, or passing down familial insight turns into a demonstration of the coherence of personality, encouraging an association among over a significant time span.

Social Festivals and Celebrations as Articulations of Personality

One of the most lively appearances of local area pride and character is tracked down in social festivals and celebrations. These occasions act as powerful articulations of a local area's qualities, convictions, and customs, giving a visual and experiential grandstand of its character. Whether it be an energetic motorcade, a customary dance execution, or a culinary celebration, these festivals become a chance for local area individuals to meet up, commend their common personality, and feature it to the more extensive world.

The demonstration of taking part in social festivals turns into an aggregate statement of personality, supporting a feeling of solidarity and pride. It is during these minutes that local area individuals commend their common legacy as well as attest their presence in the more extensive cultural woven artwork. The varieties, sounds, and kinds of these festivals become a living demonstration of the wealth and variety implanted locally's character.

Tourist spots and Images: Anchors of Personality

Tourist spots and images go about as visual anchors that encapsulate the soul and character of a local area. From notorious structures and landmarks to nearby seals and banners, these images act as unmistakable portrayals of the qualities and history that characterize a local area. The demonstration of energizing around these tourist spots encourages an aggregate pride, as local area individuals find in them an impression of their common character.

Nearby milestones frequently convey verifiable importance, filling in as standards that interface the present to the past. Whether it be a town square, a noteworthy structure, or a characteristic milestone, the protection and festivity of these actual encapsulations of personality become a common obligation. Local area individuals invest heavily in their upkeep and praise their reality, as they act as steady tokens of the aggregate excursion and legacy.

Sports and Local area Personality: Binding together Through Shared Accomplishments

In numerous networks, sports become a strong road for communicating and supporting a feeling of personality. The neighborhood sports group frequently rises above the domain of games, turning into an image of local area pride and solidarity. The demonstration of wearing group tones, going to games, and energetically supporting the neighborhood group turns into an aggregate articulation of personality, cultivating a common story of wins and difficulties.

The outcome of a nearby games group can significantly affect local area pride. Accomplishments on the field become shared triumphs, with the whole local area energizing behind their competitors. The demonstration of going to games or games turns into a public encounter, where people discover a feeling of having a place in the common cheers and festivities. The outcome of the group becomes interwoven with the local area's character, making getting through recollections and a wellspring of pride that stretches out past the donning field.

Instruction and Information as Mainstays of Personality

The quest for instruction and information frames a basic mainstay of local area character. Nearby instructive establishments, whether schools, schools, or colleges, add to molding the aggregate personality by conferring values, encouraging a feeling of local area obligation, and planning people to contribute definitively to society. The demonstration of going to these establishments turns into a common encounter that ties local area individuals together.

The character of a local area frequently tracks down articulation in its obligation to schooling and scholarly pursuits. The foundation of libraries, social focuses, and scholarly discussions turns into a demonstration of the local area's commitment to information. The demonstration of supporting instructive drives and celebrating scholarly accomplishments turns into a wellspring of aggregate pride, as the local area puts resources into the scholarly development of its individuals and the ages to come.

Difficulties and Flexibility: Manufacturing Personality Through Difficulty

The genuine strength of local area personality is much of the time uncovered despite difficulties and difficulty. Whether it be financial difficulties, cataclysmic events, or social disturbances, the manner in which a local area explores and defeats these difficulties turns into a characterizing section in its story. The demonstration of confronting misfortune together encourages a profound feeling of strength and solidarity, adding to an aggregate personality fashioned in the cauldron of shared battles.

Networks that have endured storms, both figurative and strict, frequently discover a recharged deep satisfaction in their capacity to remain steadfast notwithstanding misfortune. The narratives of strength become a piece of the common fables, went down through ages as a demonstration of the dauntless soul of the local area.

The demonstration of supporting each other, reconstructing together, and arising more grounded turns into a wellspring of getting through pride, forming the local area's way of life as one set apart by diligence and shared assurance.

Inclusivity and Variety: Expanding the Woven artwork of Character

As people group develop and adjust to the intricacies of the advanced world, the thought of character grows to embrace inclusivity and variety. The demonstration of inviting people from different foundations, societies, and points of view turns into a cognizant work to enhance the local area's personality. Comprehensive practices and festivities of variety add to a more extensive and dynamic feeling of character that mirrors the worldwide interconnectedness of contemporary society.

The demonstration of embracing variety goes past simple resistance; it turns into a functioning affirmation of the commitments of people from changed foundations. Social trades, interfaith coordinated efforts, and drives that celebrate contrasts become necessary to the local area's character. The story of character, when established in homogeneity, develops into a multi-layered embroidery that mirrors the mosaic of human encounters.

The Job of Authority in Molding Character

Authority, whether at the local area level or inside unambiguous foundations, assumes a urgent part in forming and building up a local area's personality. Visionary pioneers articulate a story that resounds with the qualities and yearnings of the local area, giving a guide to aggregate development. The demonstration of initiative turns into a cognizant work to encourage pride, solidarity, and a feeling of direction among local area individuals.

Comprehensive and sympathetic initiative turns into an impetus for building a positive and versatile local area personality. Pioneers who focus on coordinated effort, pay attention to different voices, and champion the aggregate government assistance add to a climate where people feel seen and heard. The demonstration of initiative stretches out past managerial obligations; it turns into a pledge to sustaining a feeling of having a place and divided personality between local area individuals.

The Always Advancing Embroidered artwork

All, locally pride and character are dynamic powers that shape and are molded by the aggregate encounters, values, and yearnings of people inside a local area. The demonstration of cultivating and commending local area personality is a progressing, cooperative exertion that includes recognizing shared history, embracing social variety, supporting neighborhood tourist spots, and aggregately exploring difficulties.

The account of local area character isn't static; it advances, adjusts, and extends as networks develop and change. Inclusivity, strength, social festivals, and the supporting of instructive and sports drives add to the energetic embroidery of personality that characterizes a local area.

The demonstration of perceiving and praising these components turns into a common obligation, cultivating a profound and persevering through feeling of satisfaction that ties people together in the unpredictable and steadily developing embroidery of local area personality.

4.1. Discussion on how local hockey heroes become symbols of community pride

Nearby Hockey Legends: Images of Local area Pride and Solidarity

In the core of numerous networks, the reverberation of skates cutting across the ice and the undeniable crash of a puck meeting the rear of the net act as the soundtrack to a common energy: hockey. Inside this social embroidery, neighborhood hockey legends arise as competitors as well as images of local area pride, solidarity, and a firmly established association that rises above the limits of the arena. This conversation investigates how these neighborhood hockey legends become something other than players; they become mobilizing focuses for local area pride and wellsprings of motivation that weave people together.

The Embodiment of Hockey in Local area Character

Hockey, with its speedy nature and group elements, implants itself profoundly in the texture of numerous networks. The game turns out to be in excess of a game; it turns into a social standard that characterizes the personality of a region. The arenas where kids take their first reluctant steps in quite a while and where neighborhood associations fight for matchless quality become fields of shared association. The demonstration of going to hockey games, wearing group shirts, and rooting for neighborhood players turns into a common encounter that ties people together, cultivating a feeling of local area personality.

With regards to local area pride, hockey stands apart as a binding together power. Neighborhood groups, whether in humble communities or clamoring urban areas, become exemplifications of aggregate goals and shared triumphs. The demonstration of supporting a nearby hockey group, going to games with loved ones, and taking part in the overflowing cheers resounding through the field become customs that represent support for a group as well as a certification of local area personality. The neighborhood hockey legend, in this manner, ventures onto the ice not simply as a singular player but rather as a delegate of the local area's common enthusiasm and soul.

From Skating Arenas to Community Pride: The Excursion of Neighborhood Hockey Legends

The excursion of a nearby hockey legend starts on the local arenas, where kids fantasy about copying their #1 players and scoring the triumphant objective for their town. As these hopeful competitors progress through neighborhood associations and earn respect for their expertise and commitment, they quit being only people on the ice. They change into images of trust, persistence, and the potential for significance that dwells inside the local area.

The demonstration of a nearby hockey legend binding up their skates before a game turns into a public expectation — an exemplification of aggregate dreams and goals. As they skim onto the ice, the reverberations of old neighborhood cheers resonate through the field, making an unmistakable association among player and local area. The legend's accomplishments, whether in scoring pivotal objectives, driving the group to triumph, or exhibiting extraordinary sportsmanship, become shared wins that hoist local area pride.

The meaning of neighborhood hockey legends stretches out past the arena and into the more extensive local area story. The demonstration of praising these legends turns into a local area wide undertaking, with nearby media covering their accomplishments, schools respecting them as good examples, and organizations showing flags broadcasting old neighborhood pride. The legend's excursion from nearby arenas to local, and some of the time public, acknowledgment reflects the local area's aggregate rising, and their prosperity becomes entwined with the local area's own story of development, flexibility, and shared achievements.

Motivation and Desire: Neighborhood Hockey Legends as Good examples

Nearby hockey legends act as signals of motivation, particularly for the more youthful age trying to emulate their example. The demonstration of a youthful hockey devotee seeing a nearby legend's ability on the ice turns out to be something other than an observer experience — it turns into a snapshot of significant motivation. Hopeful players copy their nearby legends, in expertise improvement as well as in epitomizing the upsides of cooperation, devotion, and sportsmanship.

The legend's excursion from neighborhood arenas to potential expert associations turns into a wellspring of desire for youthful players. The demonstration of imagining oneself in the legend's skates, scoring that vital objective, and hearing the reverberating cheers of old neighborhood allies turns into a strong inspiration. Nearby hockey legends become undeniable evidence that fantasies can be acknowledged inside the local area, imparting a feeling of satisfaction and plausibility among yearning players.

The effect of these neighborhood legends stretches out past the prompt domain of hockey. The demonstration of succeeding in the game turns into a similitude for making progress through difficult work and assurance, moving youthful people to define aggressive objectives in different parts of their lives. The legend's story turns into a common account that supports the conviction that significance can rise up out of inside the local area, cultivating a culture of desire and diligence.

Local area Commitment: The Neighborhood Legend as a Bringing together Figure

Nearby hockey legends effectively draw in with the local area, enhancing their job as bringing together figures. The demonstration of taking part in local area occasions, visiting schools, and collaborating with fans changes them into receptive images of local area pride.

Their openness separates obstructions among player and ally, making a feeling of inclusivity that reinforces local area securities.

The legend's association in nearby foundations, youth projects, and local area drives turns into an augmentation of their effect past the arena. The demonstration of offering back turns into a corresponding motion that concretes the legend's place as a positive power inside the local area. The people group, thusly, responds with esteem, support, and a more profound feeling of association.

Local area commitment likewise appears during critical hockey occasions, where the demonstration of energizing around the nearby legend turns into a common encounter. Whether it's an old neighborhood player contending in a lofty competition or accomplishing an individual achievement, the local area joins in festival. The legend's victories become common triumphs, and the demonstration of supporting them turns into an outflow of aggregate pride.

Emblematic Portrayals: Shirts, Pennants, and Urban Pride

The demonstration of wearing a nearby hockey legend's shirt turns into an intense image of urban pride. Whether worn by fans going to games, showed in retail facades, or hanging gladly in homes, these shirts convey the heaviness of shared character. The demonstration of wearing the legend's number turns into a statement of faithfulness, a visual portrayal of the local area's help and confidence in the player's capacities.

Past pullovers, the demonstration of showing pennants, paintings, and public workmanship highlighting nearby hockey legends turns into a substantial festival of local area pride. The legend's picture, frozen in a snapshot of win, turns into an installation locally scene — a persevering through demonstration of the common excursion and accomplishments of the old neighborhood player. These emblematic portrayals act as everyday tokens of the legend's effect, encouraging a consistent feeling of satisfaction and solidarity.

Perfection of Progress: The Legend's Return and Local area Festivities

The zenith of a nearby hockey legend's prosperity frequently finishes in a victorious re-visitation of their old neighborhood. The demonstration of the legend getting back to the local area, with honors and accomplishments close behind, turns into a snapshot of aggregate festival. Marches, municipal gatherings, and local area wide merriments mark the legend's return as a homecoming of shared bliss and pride.

The demonstration of coordinating local area festivities for the returning legend is a demonstration of the significant effect they have on the local area. Roads fixed with cheering allies, neighborhood organizations embellished with celebratory pennants, and the legend being greeted wholeheartedly become articulations of common appreciation. The legend's prosperity isn't simply an individual accomplishment yet a mutual victory, and the demonstration of getting together to celebrate supports the profound connection among player and local area.

Inheritance and Persevering through Effect: Past the Ice

The effect of neighborhood hockey legends reaches out past their playing days, passing on an enduring inheritance that keeps on forming local area character. The demonstration of resigning a legend's pullover, naming neighborhood offices in their honor, and laying out grants in their name turns into an approach to deifying their commitments. These motions become an interminable indication of the legend's persevering through influence on the local area.

Neighborhood legends frequently progress into jobs that permit them to reward the local area that upheld them all through their profession. The demonstration of tutoring yearning players, training nearby groups, and effectively partaking in local area improvement drives turns into a continuation of their job as uplifting figures. The legend's obligation to the local area goes past the arena, adding to the general prosperity and development of the region.

Neighborhood Legends as Mainstays of Local area Pride

All in all, neighborhood hockey legends rise above the customary job of competitors — they become mainstays of local area pride, solidarity, and motivation. The demonstration of binding up skates, scoring objectives, and addressing the local area on the ice turns into a common story that reverberates with the hearts of allies.

SAM LORAY

Neighborhood legends typify the yearnings, dreams, and versatility of the local area, becoming living images of shared personality.

The meaning of these legends lies in their athletic ability as well as in the significant effect they have on the aggregate soul of the local area. From rousing the up and coming age of players to effectively captivating in local area drives, nearby legends produce associations that reach out a long ways past the bounds of the hockey arena. Their inheritance becomes interlaced with the local area's story, making an embroidery of pride, solidarity, and shared accomplishment that perseveres through ages. The demonstration of celebrating neighborhood hockey legends isn't just about the game — it is a festival of local area, of aggregate dreams, and of the persevering through force of people to motivate and join together.

4.2. Examination of the cultural and social impact of successful local hockey players on their communities

Assessment of the Social and Social Effect of Fruitful Neighborhood Hockey Players on Their People group

The domain of sports, especially hockey, has an ability to interest to mesh itself into the social and social texture of networks. At the point when a neighborhood hockey player ascends to unmistakable quality, making progress on provincial, public, or even global stages, the effect rises above the limits of the arena. This assessment digs into the complex social and social ramifications of effective neighborhood hockey players, investigating how their accomplishments resound a long ways past the field, molding the character, values, and interconnectedness of their networks.

Social Importance: Hockey as a Social Standard

Hockey, profoundly implanted in the social legacy of numerous networks, stretches out past being a simple game — it turns into a social standard that mirrors the common character of a territory. The sound of skates coasting on ice, the conflict of sticks, and the thunder of the group make an ensemble that resounds with the local area's aggregate soul. Fruitful nearby hockey players, hence, become social ministers whose accomplishments raise the meaning of hockey inside the local area's story.

The demonstration of going to hockey games, whether at neighborhood arenas or bigger fields, turns into a collective encounter saturated with social practices. The shades of group pullovers, the serenades reverberating through the stands, and the common energy during urgent snapshots of the game add to the making of a social personality that stretches out a long ways past the limits of the arena. Effective nearby hockey players, by temperance of their accomplishments, enhance the social reverberation of the game, transforming it into a wellspring of shared pride and festivity.

Emblematic Portrayal: Nearby Legends as Social Symbols

At the point when a neighborhood hockey player rises to progress, they change into something beyond competitors — they become social symbols, emblematic portrayals of the local area's qualities, goals, and potential. The demonstration of seeing an old neighborhood player wear the shirt and succeed on a more extensive stage turns into a wellspring of aggregate motivation. The player's excursion from nearby arenas to public or global acknowledgment reflects the local area's own excursion of development, strength, and the quest for greatness.

The imagery appended to effective neighborhood hockey players stretches out to visual portrayals inside the local area. Pennants, wall paintings, and public workmanship highlighting these players become images of social pride. The demonstration of unmistakably showing these portrayals in broad daylight spaces fills in as an everyday sign of the local area's aggregate accomplishments and the getting through effect of their nearby legends. The players' pictures, frozen in snapshots of win, become apparatuses that add to the local area's social scene.

Accounts of Flexibility: Effective Players as Narrators

Each fruitful neighborhood hockey player conveys with them a story of versatility, assurance, and the capacity to beat difficulties. These accounts, frequently interlaced with the local area's own accounts, become incredible assets for narrating. The demonstration of describing the player's excursion — from early days on nearby arenas to accomplishing acknowledgment on a more extensive scale — turns into a common story that supports the upsides of difficult work, determination, and the potential for significance intrinsic inside the local area.

The story of versatility reaches out past the player's on-ice accomplishments to include their self-awareness and advancement. Neighborhood legends who explore difficulties, mishaps, and wins become living stories that resound with local area individuals.

The demonstration of sharing these stories, whether through media inclusion, local area occasions, or individual tales, adds to the production of a social embroidery that winds around together the player's singular process with the more extensive stories of the local area.

Generational Effect: Moving Future Players and Fans

The social effect of fruitful neighborhood hockey players stretches out to people in the future, affecting the goals and dreams of youthful players and fans. The demonstration of a youthful hockey fan seeing a neighborhood legend's accomplishments turns into a groundbreaking second — a motivation that rises above the limits of the arena. Effective players act as good examples, typifying the potential outcomes that exist inside the local area and imparting a feeling of satisfaction and desire in the more youthful age.

The effect of neighborhood legends on future players goes past the specialized parts of the game. It turns into a declaration that significance can rise up out of inside the local area, encouraging a confidence in one's true capacity. The demonstration of youthful players copying their nearby legends, both in expertise improvement and character, makes an expanding influence that adds to the social tradition of the local area. The legend's impact stretches out to the foundation of youth programs, local area associations, and drives that support the up and coming age of hockey lovers.

Local area Unification: Shared Festivals and Aggregate Bliss

The progress of neighborhood hockey players turns into an impetus for local area unification, encouraging a feeling of shared festival and aggregate happiness. The demonstration of energizing around a nearby legend, whether during critical competitions, achievement accomplishments, or homecoming festivities, turns into a collective encounter that rises above individual affiliations. The player's prosperity turns into a wellspring of pride that joins local area individuals, making a common story of win and achievement.

The demonstration of gathering together to celebrate, whether at local area occasions, marches, or nearby foundations, fortifies social securities. Fruitful neighborhood players become binding together figures whose accomplishments act as a point of convergence for common social events. The common happiness during these festivals adds to the formation of enduring recollections, building up the feeling of harmony that frames the groundwork of local area life.

Monetary Effect: Helping Neighborhood Economies

The social and social effect of fruitful nearby hockey players isn't bound to the close to home and emblematic domains — it stretches out to unmistakable monetary advantages for their networks. The demonstration of a player accomplishing acknowledgment on a public or global scale causes to notice the local area, setting out open doors for financial development. Expanded media inclusion, sponsorships, and the deluge of guests during celebratory occasions add to a lift in nearby economies.

Neighborhood organizations, regardless of whether straightforwardly connected with hockey, frequently experience expanded support during times of increased local area pride. Stock deals, ticket incomes, and the general excitement created by the outcome of nearby players add to financial feeling. The demonstration of facilitating celebratory occasions, like motorcades or homecoming functions, further intensifies financial action, helping neighborhood foundations and making a positive expanding influence all through the local area.

Urban Pride: Effective Players as Local area Diplomats

Effective neighborhood hockey players, by excellence of their accomplishments, become accepted representatives for their networks. The demonstration of addressing the local area on public or global stages lifts the player's singular profile as well as the profile of the local area itself. The people group's name becomes inseparable from progress, and the player's triumphs add to a positive picture that reaches out past the limits of the arena.

The demonstration of effective players drawing in with local area drives, admirable missions, and municipal occasions sets their job as local area representatives. Their impact arrives at past the games field, adding to the general prosperity and improvement of the local area. The pride related with having an effective neighborhood player turns into a common feeling that supports the local area's personality on a more extensive scale.

Difficulties and Obligations: Exploring Assumptions

While the social and social effect of fruitful nearby hockey players is prevalently positive, it accompanies its portion of difficulties and obligations. The demonstration of exploring uplifted assumptions, both from the local area and the more extensive public, can put extra tensions on players. The test lies in adjusting self-improvement, keeping up with mental prosperity, and satisfying the obligations that accompany being social and local area figures.

Nearby legends frequently wind up in a position where their activities and ways of behaving are examined past the arena. The demonstration of dealing with these assumptions requires a sensitive harmony between private independence and local area portrayal. Effective players should explore the obligations that accompany their social and social effect, effectively adding to the local area while additionally guaranteeing their singular prosperity.

Social Advancement: Adjusting to Changing Elements

The social and social effect of fruitful nearby hockey players isn't static — it develops and adjusts to changing elements inside the local area and the more extensive cultural scene. The demonstration of embracing social variety, encouraging inclusivity, and adjusting to advancing qualities becomes fundamental for players to keep up with their reverberation inside the local area. Effective players should explore social movements, adding to the continuous advancement of local area personality.

The demonstration of nearby legends effectively captivating with local area drives, reflecting changing cultural standards, and tending to contemporary difficulties guarantees that their effect stays applicable. The player's capacity to develop with the social scene of the local area adds to a maintained and persevering through impact. Fruitful players become essential supporters of the continuous social account, forming and being molded by the steadily advancing personality of their networks.

An Embroidery Woven with Progress and Shared Personality

All in all, the social and social effect of fruitful neighborhood hockey players is a rich embroidery woven with strings of progress, shared character, and local area pride. These players become more than competitors — they become social symbols, narrators, and local area ministers whose impact reaches out a long ways past the arena. The demonstration of making progress inside the domain of hockey adds to the social story of a local area, molding values, motivating people in the future, and encouraging a feeling of harmony that characterizes the aggregate soul.

The effect is felt not just in the cheers reverberating through the stands yet additionally in the financial feeling, urban pride, and the persevering through heritage that these players abandon. Effective neighborhood hockey players become necessary parts of the local area's story, adding to the continuous development of social character. Their accomplishments act as guides of motivation, representing the potential for significance that dwells inside the local area and rousing people to dream past the limits of the arena. In this harmonious connection among players and networks, achievement turns into a common excursion, and the social and social effect reverberations through the ages, making a heritage that gets through lengthy after the last whistle blows.

4.3. Stories of how hometowns rally behind their heroes, creating a sense of identity and unity

Accounts of Old neighborhood Pride: Joining People group Behind Their Legends

In the core of each and every old neighborhood, there exists an exceptional speculative chemistry — a combination of aggregate dreams, shared narratives, and a firmly established pride that tracks down its most impactful articulation in the outcome of nearby legends. These accounts, woven into the actual texture of networks, unfurl like an embroidery of versatility, enthusiasm, and solidarity. This investigation digs into the stories that enlighten the manners by which main residences rally behind their legends, making a significant feeling of character and solidarity that rises above the common.

The Beginning: From Neighborhood Arenas to Worldwide Stages

The stories of old neighborhood legends frequently initiate on the modest ice of nearby arenas, where the reverberation of skates against the ice fills in as a preface to an excursion that will resound a long ways past the limits of the local area.

These accounts start with the youth longs for neighborhood young people, binding up their skates in quest for an energy that will convey them to levels beforehand unheard of.

The demonstration of revitalizing behind a neighborhood legend starts in these early stages, as families, companions, and the local area in general observer the early walks of these growing competitors. Neighborhood arenas become the stage for dreams to come to fruition, and as the legends in-the-production explore the multi-faceted dance of youth associations, the local area turns into a crowd of people, by and large putting resources into the commitment of significance.

Shared Desires: A People group's Fantasies Encapsulated

As nearby legends progress in their excursions, the local area's fantasies become entwined with the desires of these competitors. The demonstration of trying for progress through the undertakings of an old neighborhood legend changes the story from individual accomplishment to a shared victory. Every objective scored, each honor procured, and the quest for greatness on territorial and public stages reverberate as shared desires, building up the conviction that the fantasies of a local area can for sure emerge.

The demonstration of revitalizing behind these competitors turns into a corresponding motion — a common interest in progress and shared personality. The people group's fantasies track down epitome in the accomplishments of their legends, making an account that stretches out past the person to turn into an aggregate story of tirelessness and win. The legends, thusly, convey the heaviness of these yearnings as they progress, understanding that their process isn't simply private yet a common odyssey that ties them to the actual substance of their old neighborhood.

Social Points of support: Legends as Images of Nearby Personality

Neighborhood legends, with their shirts embellished with old neighborhood symbols, arise as social points of support, exemplifying the novel character of their networks. The demonstration of wearing the neighborhood tones turns into a visual portrayal of aggregate personality, changing each game into a festival of the local area's uniqueness. The legends' accomplishments become inseparable from the qualities, customs, and social subtleties that characterize the places where they grew up.

The demonstration of revitalizing behind these legends takes on an emblematic importance, rising above the limits of the arena. The people group embraces its legends as competitors as well as images of versatility, trust, and the potential for significance that lives inside their middle. The legends, thus, become stewards of neighborhood personality, bearing the obligation of addressing their networks on more extensive stages with a significant comprehension of the social heritage they convey.

Local area Customs: Shared Delight in Win and Challenge

In the embroidered artwork of old neighborhood pride, local area customs unfurl as shared encounters that enhance the delights of win and give comfort even with difficulties. The demonstration of get-together at nearby foundations to watch critical games, wearing group tones during local area occasions, and all in all commending triumphs turns into a ceremonial articulation of solidarity. These customs are not just about the game; they are functions that support the local area's aggregate soul.

Wins on the ice become mutual victories, starting ejections of satisfaction that resonate through the local area. The demonstration of gathering together to celebrate, whether through improvised road social occasions or coordinated occasions, turns into a demonstration of the force of shared euphoria. On the other hand, in snapshots of challenge and rout, the local area unites behind their legends with unfaltering help, exhibiting that the common character is strong notwithstanding affliction.

The Old neighborhood Benefit: Faithful Help

The connection among main residences and their legends is portrayed by an enduring help that reaches out past the pinnacles of progress and the valleys of misfortune. The demonstration of revitalizing behind neighborhood legends isn't dependent upon the scoreline or the measurements; it is a responsibility established in the comprehension that the legends are players in a group, however encapsulations of the local area's desires.

This help appears in different structures — from neighborhood organizations showing pennants to schools sorting out occasions to pay tribute to their legends. The people group rallies to offer monetary help for youth programs, guaranteeing that the cutting edge has the assets to seek after their fantasies. The legends, thusly, feel the heaviness of this help, perceiving that each step on the ice is supported by a local area that has confidence in their true capacity.

Homecoming Festivities: A Legend's Re-visitation of Veneration

The apex of the connection among main residences and their legends frequently unfurls in the blissful exhibition of homecoming festivities. The demonstration of the legend getting back to their underlying foundations, decorated with honors and accomplishments, turns into a collective occasion that rises above the conventional. Roads fixed with cheering allies, neighborhood organizations enhanced with standards, and the legend being greeted wholeheartedly become articulations of shared veneration.

The demonstration of sorting out homecoming festivities is a significant statement of the local area's pride and appreciation for their legends. The legends, thus, are not simply getting back to the places where they grew up; they are getting back to where their triumphs are appreciated, and their process is viewed as basic to the local area's story. Homecoming festivities become a demonstration of the persevering through effect of the legends on the actual texture of the places where they grew up.

Generational Accounts: Passing the Light of Motivation

The tales of main residences energizing behind their legends stretch out past the current second — they become stories that rouse people in the future. The demonstration of a youthful hockey lover seeing the praise and backing showered upon a nearby legend turns into a seed of motivation. Yearning players, powered by the fantasies of their ancestors, trim up their skates with the comprehension that the arena isn't simply a landmark; it is a phase where the stories of their old neighborhood legends unfurl.

The legends, mindful of their jobs as motivations, effectively draw in with youth projects, schools, and local area occasions. They become guides, passing on the specialized abilities of the game as well as the upsides of tirelessness, sportsmanship, and local area commitment. The demonstration of supporting the goals of the cutting edge turns into a persevering through heritage, guaranteeing that the tales of old neighborhood pride keep on being composed by new parts of legends.

Social Advancement: Embracing Variety and Inclusivity

The stories of old neighborhood pride are dynamic, adjusting to changing social scenes and embracing variety. The demonstration of mobilizing behind legends turns into a festival of inclusivity, where players from various foundations, nationalities, and characters end up embraced by the aggregate personality of the local area. Main residences develop with the times, recognizing that the strength of their personality lies in the lavishness of variety.

Neighborhood legends, in their jobs as social envoys, effectively add to this social development. They take part in drives that advance inclusivity, separate boundaries, and encourage a feeling of having a place for everybody locally. The demonstration of embracing variety turns into an essential piece of the old neighborhood pride account, guaranteeing that the legends' accounts reverberate with a consistently growing crowd.

Difficulties and Solidarity: Facing the Hardship Together

The accounts of old neighborhood pride are not safe to challenges, and the demonstration of revitalizing behind legends is tried in snapshots of difficulty. Whether confronting a terrible streak, discussions, or outer tensions, the local area's obligation to its legends is a demonstration of the persevering through strength of the bond. In the midst of challenge, the legends find comfort in the information that they are in good company — the places where they grew up stand by them, unflinching in their help.

The provokes become open doors for the local area to show its flexibility and solidarity. The demonstration of enduring tempests together, be it on the ice or despite outer reactions, supports the aggregate soul of old neighborhood pride. The legends, thus, find recharged assurance, understanding that their processes are shared stories that rise above individual accomplishments.

An Orchestra of Shared Character and Aggregate Flexibility

All in all, the tales of main residences mobilizing behind their legends unfurl as an ensemble — an amicable mix of shared personality, aggregate flexibility, and the getting through pride that exudes from the core of networks. These accounts go past the game of hockey; they become social inheritances, restricting ages together through the strings of shared dreams and aggregate victories.

The demonstration of mobilizing behind neighborhood legends is a festival of the pith that makes every old neighborhood exceptional. It is a demonstration of the force of solidarity, the strength got from shared goals, and the getting through connection among networks and their legends. These accounts, scratched into the social scenes of main residences, act as signals of motivation, showing the significant effect that people can have on the aggregate soul of a local area.

In the embroidery of old neighborhood pride, each step on the ice turns into a note in a tune that resounds through the hearts of allies. The legends, hung in the shades of the places where they grew up, convey the heaviness of aggregate dreams, and in their excursions, they make stories that reverberation through ages. Main residences and legends, in their solidarity, make a story that rises above time — an account that celebrates the triumphs on the scoreboard as well as the persevering through soul of networks that track down strength in the tales of their own.

Main residences Rally Behind Their Legends: A Binding together Power

In the complex embroidery of nearby networks, there exists a strong peculiarity — an aggregate soul that arises when main residences rally behind their legends. These legends, frequently arising out of the actual texture of the local area, become more than simple competitors; they develop into images of shared personality, strength, and pride. The demonstration of revitalizing behind these old neighborhood legends is a significant articulation of local area solidarity, fashioning bonds that reach out a long ways past the limits of sports fields.

At the core of this mobilizing is the common excursion that unfurls on neighborhood arenas. From the early desires of growing competitors to the victories accomplished on provincial and public stages, the local area observes the advancement of their legends. The legends, thus, perceive the heaviness of aggregate assumptions and desires that go with all their steps, understanding that they are playing for individual brilliance as well as are stewards of the local area's fantasies.

The demonstration of revitalizing behind old neighborhood legends turns into a proportional relationship, a common interest in progress that is strengthened by a profound feeling of shared goals. Every objective scored, each honor procured, and the quest for greatness turns into a collective victory, building up the conviction that the fantasies of a local area can emerge.

The legends typify the social mainstays of the places where they grew up, wearing shirts decorated with nearby badges that represent a group as well as the qualities, customs, and subtleties that characterize the local area.

Local area ceremonies assume a urgent part in the story of revitalizing behind legends. Whether gathering at nearby foundations to observe significant games or on the whole praising triumphs, these customs become services of solidarity. Wins on the ice are met with emissions of collective euphoria that resonate through the local area, while snapshots of challenge and rout see the local area coming together for their legends with enduring help. The connection among main residences and legends is portrayed by a persevering through help that rises above scorelines, insights, and individual exhibitions.

Homecoming festivities stand as apex minutes in the connection among main residences and legends. The legends, getting back to their underlying foundations embellished with honors and accomplishments, are greeted wholeheartedly in a cheerful exhibition that changes the roads into a material of collective love. These festivals are not just about the legends; they are about the local area reaffirming its pride and appreciation for the basic job their legends play in the social story.

The effect of old neighborhood mobilizing reaches out past the current second — it turns into a generational story, moving future legends and lovers. The accounts of neighborhood legends passing the light of motivation to the cutting edge unfurl as seeds of desire established in the hearts of yearning players. Legends, in their jobs as coaches, effectively draw in with youth projects, schools, and local area occasions, adding to the social heritage and guaranteeing that the tales of old neighborhood pride keep on advancing.

In the unique scene of social advancement, main residences embrace variety and inclusivity through their legends. The demonstration of mobilizing behind competitors from various foundations, nationalities, and personalities turns into a festival of the extravagance of variety inside the local area. Old neighborhood legends, filling in as social diplomats, effectively add to this development by taking part in drives that advance inclusivity and cultivate a feeling of having a place for everybody.

Moves become open doors for main residences to show their solidarity and flexibility. Whether confronting a terrible streak, contentions, or outer tensions, the local area's obligation to its legends is resolute. In the midst of challenge, the legends find comfort in the information that they are in good company — the places where they grew up stand by them, supporting the aggregate soul of old neighborhood pride.

The demonstration of main residences revitalizing behind their legends is an orchestra — an amicable mix of shared personality, aggregate versatility, and getting through pride. These stories go past the actual game, becoming social inheritances that tight spot ages together through the strings of shared dreams and wins. The legends, hung in the shades of the places where they grew up, convey the heaviness of aggregate dreams, and in their excursions, they make stories that reverberation through ages. Main residences and legends, in their solidarity, make a story that rises above time — an account that celebrates the triumphs on the scoreboard as well as the getting through soul of networks that track down strength in the narratives of their own.

Chapter 5

Challenges and Triumphs

Difficulties and Wins: Exploring the Perplexing Territory of Sports and Then some

In the domain of sports, difficulties and wins are the double powers that shape the accounts of competitors, groups, and whole networks. The excursion from neighborhood arenas to public or global stages is full of deterrents that request strength, assurance, and the capacity to explore intricacies past the scoreboard. This investigation dives into the diverse scene of difficulties and wins, unwinding the many-sided strings that weave the narratives of competitors and groups in the powerful universe of sports.

The Capricious Territory of Rivalry

At the core of each and every athletic undertaking lies the capricious territory of rivalry. Challenges manifest as considerable rivals, key vulnerabilities, and the consistently present strain to perform at top levels. Competitors and groups wind up exploring this landscape, where wins are in many cases hard-faced conflicts against affliction.

The difficulties introduced by adversaries are not just physical; they stretch out to the psychological and close to home elements of contest. Competitors should wrestle with the mental part of confronting imposing enemies, translating their systems, and keeping a psychological guts that endures the tensions of high-stakes rivalries.

Wins on the cutthroat stage, in this way, become impressions of actual ability as well as of mental strength and key keenness.

Physical and Mental Strength: The Cauldron of Difficulties

The actual requests of sports force difficulties that test the restrictions of a competitor's perseverance, strength, and deftness. Wounds, weariness, and the afflictions of serious preparation regimens become imposing enemies on the way to win. Competitors should explore the sensitive harmony between pushing their actual limits and shielding their prosperity, frequently going with split-subsequent options that influence their singular exhibition as well as the aggregate outcome of the group.

Similarly critical is the psychological strength expected to face difficulties that rise above the actual domain. Competitors face the steady examination of public assumptions, the heaviness of past exhibitions, and the steady strain to convey predictable greatness. Wins notwithstanding such mental difficulties become emblematic triumphs over self-question, outer tensions, and the mental cost of the cutthroat field.

Versatility: Exploring Changing Tides

The scene of sports is portrayed by its dynamic nature — continually developing standards, techniques, and outside factors that request flexibility. Competitors and groups should explore the changing tides of their particular games, changing procedures, embracing development, and remaining on the ball. Wins in such a climate are frequently credited to the capacity to adjust, improve, and decisively position oneself in the steadily moving flows of sports elements.

Outside factors, including mechanical headways, rule changes, and changes in training ways of thinking, present difficulties that request clever versatility. Competitors who can outfit these progressions for their potential benefit, consolidating new methods or utilizing headways in sports science, frequently wind up at the front of wins. The capacity to see difficulties as any open doors for development and transformation turns into a sign of persevering through progress.

Group Elements: The Aggregate Victories and Afflictions

For group activities, provokes reach out past individual exhibitions to the unpredictable elements of group joint effort. Wins are in many cases aggregate accomplishments, requiring consistent coordination, powerful correspondence, and a common obligation to a shared objective. Challenges inside the group dynamic might emerge from contrasts in playing styles, relational struggles, or the inborn strain to convey as a durable unit.

Initiative inside the group turns into a basic consider exploring difficulties and guiding the aggregate toward win. Skippers, mentors, and compelling colleagues should encourage a positive group culture, ingrain a feeling of solidarity, and address clashes with vital discretion.

Wins inside the group dynamic are tied in with winning matches as well as about manufacturing bonds that endure the cauldron of difficulties, making a tough and strong unit that rises above individual commitments.

Wounds: The Inconspicuous Foes

Quite possibly of the most impressive test in the realm of sports is the phantom of wounds — a tenacious foe that can sideline competitors and groups, disturbing the fragile equilibrium between wins and difficulties. The actual cost of sports, with its high-influence developments and extraordinary preparation regimens, conveys wounds an inescapable intimidation. Competitors should battle with the chance of misfortunes, restoration, and the psychological strength expected to conquer the actual constraints forced by wounds.

Wins over wounds are demonstrations of the flexibility of competitors. The excursion from injury to recuperation includes actual restoration as well as a psychological and profound fight to recover certainty and return to maximized operation. Competitors who effectively explore this difficult territory frequently arise more grounded, furnished with an increased appreciation for their actual prosperity and a restored assurance to win over misfortune.

Media Examination: The Situation with two sides

In a time of extreme media inclusion and moment network, competitors face the two sided deal of media examination. The difficulties presented by steady open consideration, web-based entertainment discourse, and the strain to keep a positive public picture can be huge. Competitors should explore the sensitive equilibrium of safeguarding their confidential lives while fulfilling the requests of a crowd of people hungry for bits of knowledge into their characters, ways of life, and exhibitions.

Wins over media investigation include on-field victories as well as the capacity to develop a positive public picture, draw in with fans, and endure analysis with beauty. Competitors who succeed in overseeing media relations frequently find themselves celebrated for their athletic accomplishments as well as appreciated for their capacity to explore the difficulties of public openness.

Monetary Tensions: Adjusting Enthusiasm and Job

While the quest for sports is frequently filled by enthusiasm, competitors should likewise battle with the monetary tensions that accompany a lifelong in elite athletics. Contract discussions, underwriting bargains, and the unstable idea of sports industry financial aspects present difficulties that require monetary keenness and key preparation. Wins in the monetary domain include getting rewarding agreements as well as going with informed choices that protected long haul monetary dependability.

The crossing point of enthusiasm and job turns into a fragile equilibrium that competitors should explore. The difficulties of monetary tensions can affect mental prosperity, with competitors wrestling with the assumptions for monetary accomplishment close by the quest for their athletic objectives. Wins in overseeing monetary tensions include tracking down balance, settling on sound monetary choices, and guaranteeing that the energy for the game remaining parts undiminished regardless of the intricacies of the monetary scene.

Social Obligation: The Call to Have an Effect

In a period where competitors are progressively viewed as compelling figures past the domain of sports, the call for social obligation presents the two difficulties and open doors. Competitors are in many cases pushed into the spotlight as promoters for social causes, expecting them to explore complex cultural issues. The difficulties include offsetting individual convictions with public assumptions, tending to analysis, and dealing with the likely reaction of taking a position on hostile issues.

Wins in the domain of social obligation include involving one's foundation for positive effect, affecting change, and adding to significant cultural talk. Competitors who effectively explore these difficulties become images of athletic ability as well as persuasive voices for social change, utilizing their victories to enhance significant makes and move others have an effect.

The Job of Wins in Beating Difficulties: A Story of Motivation

Wins, inside the setting of sports, take on a significant importance past the scoreboard. They become accounts of motivation, stories that rise above the field of play and resound with crowds a long ways past the bounds of arenas. The capacity of competitors and groups to win over difficulties turns into an encouraging sign, a demonstration of the dauntless human soul, and a wellspring of inspiration for people confronting their own misfortunes.

The unpredictable exchange among difficulties and wins characterizes the embodiment of sports. The excursion from nearby arenas to worldwide stages includes exploring capricious landscapes, defying physical and mental foes, adjusting to evolving elements, and beating impediments that stretch out past the limits of sports fields. Wins, subsequently, become markers of triumph as well as stories of versatility, motivation, and the getting through human ability to defeat difficulties. In the powerful universe of sports, the tales of wins and moves keep on enrapturing crowds, advising us that, past the quest for triumph, lies a story of human steadiness that rises above the transient idea of wins and misfortunes.

5.1. Exploration of the challenges faced by local hockey players in their journey to the top

Investigation of Difficulties in the Excursion of Neighborhood Hockey Players to the Zenith of Accomplishment

The excursion of neighborhood hockey players from the grassroots level to the zenith of progress is a story set apart by difficulties that shape their personality, versatility, and assurance. This investigation dives into the multi-layered difficulties looked by these competitors, unwinding the intricacies that go with the quest for greatness in the profoundly aggressive universe of hockey.

Grassroots Difficulties: The Underpinning of the Excursion

At the grassroots level, where dreams flourish, challenges arise as basic parts of a player's turn of events. Restricted admittance to quality instructing, hardware, and offices presents jumps that hopeful players should explore. The shortfall of organized youth programs and serious associations can block the early advancement of abilities, compelling players to depend on crude ability and an intrinsic enthusiasm for the game.

Monetary imperatives frequently add an extra layer of intricacy to the grassroots difficulties. Numerous youthful players and their families face the weight of funding gear, travel costs, and support charges. The financial boundaries can excessively influence players from oppressed foundations, restricting their admittance to open doors and preventing the possible disclosure of dormant ability.

Contest and Determination: The Pot of Ability Recognizable proof

As players progress through youth associations and school contests, they experience the pot of ability recognizable proof — a stage set apart by extraordinary rivalry and the test of standing apart in the midst of a pool of trying competitors. Mentors and scouts entrusted with recognizing potential ability face the troublesome errand of offsetting crude expertise with the intangibles that characterize a player's expected commitment to a group.

The test of being chosen or explored frequently reaches out past on-ice execution. Factors like disposition, hard working attitude, and versatility become necessary contemplations, adding layers of intricacy to the choice cycle. Numerous gifted players might end up disregarded because of elements unchangeable as far as they might be concerned, enhancing the misfortune looked on the excursion to acknowledgment and progression.

Exploring Youth Associations: The Battle for Perceivability

Youth associations act as favorable places for ability, however the battle for perceivability inside these associations presents a critical test. Restricted openness and acknowledgment can block a player's possibilities being explored by more elevated level groups or lofty improvement programs. The absence of a normalized exploring framework and the emotional idea of ability assessment further compound the hardships looked by players looking for potential chances to progress in their hockey professions.

The strain to perform reliably in youth associations can likewise negatively affect youthful players. Adjusting scholarly responsibilities, prevailing difficulties, and the requests of cutthroat hockey requires a degree of development and time-usage abilities that can be trying for players still in the developmental phases of their turn of events.

Progress to Junior Associations: A More extreme Trip

The progress from youth to junior associations addresses an essential crossroads in a player's excursion, set apart by a more extreme trip and elevated contest. Junior associations act as a critical venturing stone to more significant levels of play, including school hockey or passage into proficient associations. Notwithstanding, the difficulties become more articulated, with the force of play, actual requests, and the stakes of execution rising fundamentally.

Players face the test of adjusting to the quicker pace and expanded genuineness of junior associations. The serious scene turns out to be more merciless, with players competing for restricted program spots in groups that act as pipelines to university or expert open doors. The strain to grab the eye of school scouts or expert groups increases, putting extra weight on players exploring this basic period of their vocations.

Scholastic and Vocation Difficult exercise: Shuffling Double Needs

For some nearby hockey players, the quest for their athletic dreams is joined by the test of adjusting scholastic responsibilities and, in the end, potential profession desires. The requests of junior and school level hockey frequently expect players to travel broadly, missing huge lumps of the scholarly year. Exploring this scholarly athletic difficult exercise requires an elevated degree of discipline, using time productively, and support from instructive organizations.

The test of keeping up with scholastic execution turns out to be much more articulated as players try to contend at the university level. School hockey programs frequently request a thorough responsibility both on and off the ice, requiring a sensitive balance between wearing greatness and scholarly obligations. The tensions of protecting a school grant or offsetting scholastics with a potential expert vocation add layers of intricacy to the excursion.

Monetary Strain: The Significant expense of Seeking after Dreams

Monetary difficulties persevere as a dependable friend all through the excursion of neighborhood hockey players. The expenses related with movement, hardware, pre-paring projects, and investment charges can put a critical weight on players and their families. Junior and school level hockey frequently accompany significant monetary responsibilities, including educational expenses, which can restrict admittance to potential open doors for players from monetarily hindered foundations.

The monetary strain stretches out past private costs to the more extensive biological system of youth and junior hockey associations.

A large number of these associations work on limited financial plans, depending on sponsorships, gifts, and gathering pledges endeavors to support programs. The monetary difficulties looked by neighborhood hockey players are interconnected with the more extensive financial real factors of the game, making a complicated scene that requests intelligent fixes to guarantee inclusivity and openness.

Injury Mishaps: The Unusual Obstructions

In the genuinely requesting universe of hockey, injury difficulties arise as capricious hindrances that can crash even the most encouraging vocations. Players face the steady gamble of wounds going from minor difficulties to more serious, possibly profession adjusting conditions. The test lies in recuperating from wounds as well as in exploring the psychological and close to home cost that goes with actual difficulties.

Injury recovery requests a huge responsibility of time and assets, and players frequently wind up wrestling with the anxiety toward lost open doors and the strain to recapture top state of being. Beating the mental obstacles related with wounds turns into a fundamental piece of the excursion, requiring flexibility, persistence, and an emotionally supportive network to explore the difficulties presented by the erratic idea of sports-related wounds.

Exploring the University Scene: A Perplexing Enrollment Cycle

For the individuals who seek to play school hockey, the enlistment interaction adds a layer of intricacy to the excursion. Players face the test of promoting themselves to school mentors, displaying their abilities, and standing apart in the midst of a serious pool of volunteers. The enlistment interaction includes on-ice execution as well as powerful correspondence, self-promotion, and the capacity to explore the subtleties of university sports programs.

The test of getting a school grant includes investigating and recognizing programs that line up with the player's intellectual and athletic objectives. Exploring the complexities of NCAA guidelines, understanding grant offers, and settling on informed conclusions about university responsibilities become critical parts of the excursion. The tensions related with the enlistment interaction add one more aspect to the difficulties looked by nearby hockey players trying to play at the university level.

Progress to Proficient Associations: The Climax of an Excursion

For the limited handful who explore the provokes and secure chances to play expertly, the excursion arrives at its summit. Changing to proficient associations presents another arrangement of difficulties, including the raised degree of rivalry, the requests of an exhausting timetable, and the strain to perform at the most elevated level. Players should adjust to the business part of pro athletics, overseeing agreements, supports, and the eccentricism of group elements.

The monetary contemplations at the expert level bring the two open doors and difficulties. While fruitful experts can accomplish monetary strength through pay rates, supports, and worthwhile agreements, the serious idea of pro athletics requests predictable execution to get long haul vocations. Players face the test of exploring a dynamic and frequently flighty expert scene, where factors like exchanges, wounds, and group elements can impact the direction of their vocations.

Psychological wellness: The Quiet Test

All through the excursion, the frequently ignored challenge of psychological well-being poses a potential threat. The tensions, assumptions, and vulnerabilities innate chasing a hockey profession can negatively affect the psychological prosperity of players. From the pressure of rivalry and the apprehension about inability to the difficulties of adjusting double needs and confronting the unconventionality of wounds, players might wrestle with tension, sorrow, or other psychological well-being issues.

Tending to psychological well-being difficulties requires a social shift inside the hockey local area, encouraging a climate that focuses on the prosperity of players. Perceiving the indications of emotional well-being battles, diminishing the shame related with looking for help, and offering sufficient help frameworks are fundamental parts of making a comprehensive way to deal with the difficulties looked by nearby hockey players.

A Strong Excursion Set apart by Wins Over Difficulties

The excursion of neighborhood hockey players to the zenith of progress is a strong story set apart by wins over a heap of difficulties. From the grassroots level to proficient fields, players should explore monetary requirements, contest, injury difficulties, scholastic obligations, and the flighty idea of sports. The difficulties are basic to the fashioning of character, versatility, and assurance that characterize effective competitors.

While every player's process is special, the aggregate story mirrors the persevering through soul of the individuals who defeat impediments to understand their hockey dreams. The difficulties looked by nearby hockey players highlight the requirement for a complete and comprehensive way to deal with youth and junior improvement programs, underscoring openness, monetary help, and emotional well-being assets. Eventually, the victories over challenges become symbolic of the unstoppable human soul that pushes competitors from nearby arenas to the stupendous phases of hockey achievement.

5.2. Stories of triumph over adversity and the resilience displayed by these players

Accounts of Win over Affliction: The Strength of Nearby Hockey Players

The universe of hockey is packed with rousing accounts of win over affliction, displaying the faithful versatility of nearby players who confronted impressive provokes on their excursions to progress. These accounts go past the scoresheets and feature the dauntless soul that pushes competitors to defeat deterrents, reclassify their cutoff points, and arise as guides of motivation for hopeful players and fans the same.

From Humble Starting points to Hockey Magnificence: A Story of Steadfast Assurance

One such story of win starts in the core of an unassuming community, where a youthful player found an enthusiasm for hockey with negligible assets. Experiencing childhood in a monetarily tested climate, this player confronted the double difficulties of restricted admittance to quality training and monetary imperatives that might have smothered the quest for their fantasies. In any case, the player's unflinching assurance and love for the game impelled them to track down clever fixes.

Courageous by the absence of organized youth programs, this hopeful competitor looked for direction from nearby guides, consumed each piece of hockey astuteness accessible, and leveled up their abilities on stopgap arenas. The monetary obstacles were met with cleverness — acquired gear, local area support, and raising money endeavors that supported the player's process as well as touched off a feeling of kinship inside the town.

As the player advanced through youth and junior associations, their strength became apparent in each difficulty changed into a chance for development. Wounds that might have wrecked the excursion were met with restrained restoration, displaying actual ability as well as a psychological courage that would not capitulate to misfortune. The town mobilized behind their nearby legend, coordinating pledge drives and local area occasions to guarantee that monetary limitations didn't obstruct the player's climb.

The peak of this story unfurls as the player gets a school grant, a finish of long periods of persistence, penance, and a strong soul. The excursion from humble starting points to the university level turns into a demonstration of the groundbreaking force of assurance, local area support, and a tireless quest for energy. This player's story reverberates as an individual victory as well as a guide for others confronting comparative difficulties, showing that the human soul can take off in spite of the heaviness of difficulty.

Beating Social Hindrances: A Victory of Variety and Incorporation

In one more corner of the hockey world, a player confronted difficulties that reached out past the arena — social hindrances that might have smothered their fantasies. Experiencing childhood locally where hockey was not the prevailing game and social assumptions frequently veered from the quest for an athletic vocation, this player explored the sensitive harmony among custom and enthusiasm.

The underlying opposition from family and local area to the unusual decision of chasing after hockey turned into a pot of character for this player. In a scene where variety in sports was not the standard, the excursion included beating actual rivals on the ice as well as dissipating assumptions about social assumptions. The player turned into a pioneer, testing generalizations and motivating another age to embrace variety in sports.

Win came not just in that frame of mind of individual accomplishment on the ice yet in the more extensive social shift saw inside the local area. The player's process ignited discussions about inclusivity, separating hindrances that confined admittance to hockey in light of social foundations. The once-distrustful local area became intense allies, celebrating the player's triumphs as well as the more extensive victory of variety and consideration in a game that rises above social limits.

The strength showed in this story isn't just about conquering actual difficulties however about exploring the perplexing elements of social assumptions. The player's victory turns into a living demonstration of the influence of variety in enhancing the texture of hockey and making a more comprehensive and inviting local area.

From Difficulties to Fame: An Excursion of Reclamation

A few accounts of win over misfortune are characterized by difficulties that might have denoted the finish of a player's vocation however rather became venturing stones to fame. In one such story, a skilled player confronted a progression of sad occasions — a profession undermining injury, a line of group changes, and individual difficulties that appeared to be unfavorable. As opposed to capitulating to surrender, this player transformed misfortune into an impetus for individual and expert development.

The excursion of reclamation started in the restoration room, where the player recuperated truly as well as developed mental flexibility. The injury, as opposed to being a barrier, turned into a chance for thoughtfulness and a restored obligation to the game. The player looked for mentorship, embraced sports brain science, and arose out of the restoration more grounded, both genuinely and intellectually.

Group changes, frequently saw as weakening, turned into an essential move in this player's story. Each new group introduced a chance for reexamination, exhibiting versatility and a promise to contributing emphatically to the group dynamic.

Instead of being characterized by misfortunes, the player's story moved to one of tireless assurance and a refusal to allow conditions to direct the direction of their profession.

Individual difficulties, whether coming from connections or outside pressures, became fuel for self-disclosure and development. The player vanquished the difficulties as well as changed them into wellsprings of motivation. Through weakness and receptiveness about their excursion, the player turned into a coach for others confronting comparable misfortunes, demonstrating that strength isn't just about beating difficulties yet about involving them as venturing stones to arrive at new levels.

Win Over Separation: Breaking the Discriminatory constraint

In the more extensive setting of hockey, accounts of win over affliction likewise incorporate those that challenge fundamental segregation and hindrances inside the game. A player, confronting separation in light of orientation, transcended the bias as well as turned into a pioneer in breaking the discriminatory limitation for ladies in hockey.

This player's process included going up against orientation generalizations, engaging predispositions, and demonstrating that ability and enthusiasm are not bound by orientation. Despite difficulty, the player upheld for orientation uniformity, rousing strategy changes inside associations and cultivating a culture of inclusivity. The excursion from being underestimated to turning into a reference point for hopeful female players encapsulates the victory of flexibility against foundational challenges.

The player's story goes past private accomplishment to catalyze a development for value and portrayal. The victory isn't only individual however an aggregate triumph that resounds through the hockey local area, flagging a shift towards a more comprehensive and evenhanded future for the game.

The Embroidery of Versatility Woven in Hockey's Accounts

The narratives of win over difficulty in the realm of hockey structure a rich embroidery woven with strings of flexibility, assurance, and the unwavering soul of neighborhood players. These stories go past the limits of the arena, delineating that win isn't just about triumph on the scoreboard however about conquering individual, social, and fundamental difficulties.

Whether rising up out of humble starting points, testing social assumptions, exploring difficulties, or breaking obstructions, these players epitomize the embodiment of versatility. Their processes motivate hopeful competitors as well as add to the more extensive story of hockey as a game that rises above limits and embraces the victories that emerge from the aggregate versatility of its players.

These accounts act as a demonstration of the persevering through soul of hockey players who, even with misfortune, pick not exclusively to get by however to flourish.

They become living encapsulations of the possibility that genuine victory lies in dominating matches as well as in the excursion of versatility, development, and the tenacious quest for one's energy despite everything.

Win Over Difficulty and the Flexibility of the Human Soul: A Story of Mental fortitude and Constancy

The account of win over misfortune is a getting through demonstration of the unstoppable human soul, displaying the remarkable limit of people to transcend difficulties and arise more grounded. This story of versatility is woven with strings of mental fortitude, assurance, and an enduring obligation to defeat obstructions that, on occasion, appeared to be unrealistic.

The Cauldron of Misfortune: A Proving Ground for Character

Misfortune frequently fills in as a cauldron, testing the backbone of people and manufacturing their personality in the flames of difficulties. Whether confronted with individual mishaps, proficient obstacles, or surprising life turns, the underlying effect of difficulty can overpower. Notwithstanding, it is inside this pot that the seeds of versatility are planted, standing by to develop and develop in the midst of the wild territory of difficulties.

Despite difficulty, people frequently experience a vital crossroads — a valuable chance to face their feelings of trepidation, embrace inconvenience, and channel their internal strength. The cauldron turns into a space for self-revelation, driving people to deal with their weaknesses and restrictions. This course of contemplation and mindfulness establishes the groundwork for the versatility that will direct them through the turbulent excursion of win.

Impetuses for Win: Transforming Difficulties into Springboards

Win over misfortune is certainly not a straight way however a progression of pinnacles and valleys, interspersed by mishaps that can either crash or impel people forward. The impetus for win frequently lies in the capacity to transform mishaps into springboards for development. Rather than capitulating to the heaviness of difficulties, versatile people influence mishaps as any open doors for learning, variation, and change.

One of the critical impetuses for win is a change in context — a reevaluating of difficulties as venturing stones as opposed to unrealistic hindrances. This mental shift engages people to see misfortune as a characteristic piece of the excursion, recognizing that mishaps are not signs of disappointment yet rather markers of flexibility really taking shape. The capacity to remove illustrations from mishaps turns into a powerful instrument for exploring the intricacies of life.

Also, win over misfortune is much of the time energized by a resolute assurance to endure notwithstanding the chances.

This assurance goes about as a main impetus that impels people forward, in any event, when the way appears to be challenging. The strength to persevere through difficulties, to continue moving notwithstanding mishaps, turns into a principal quality that isolates win from rout.

The Job of Emotionally supportive networks: A Mainstay of Solidarity

While individual strength is principal, the job of emotionally supportive networks couldn't possibly be more significant in that frame of mind of win over difficulty. Family, companions, tutors, and networks frequently act as mainstays of solidarity during testing times. The force of human association and the help got from certifiable connections make a wellbeing net that mellow the falls and gives a take off platform to inevitable victory.

Emotionally supportive networks offer close to home food, giving a space to people to communicate weaknesses, fears, and questions without judgment. The demonstration of imparting one's battles to a believed partner cultivates a feeling of fellowship and supports the comprehension that strength is definitely not a single undertaking however a cooperative excursion.

Past consistent reassurance, substantial help from emotionally supportive networks can likewise assume an essential part. Whether as monetary guide, viable help, or basically listening carefully, the aggregate strength of a steady local area turns into an encouraging sign during the most obscure snapshots of difficulty. The affirmation that one isn't the only one in their battles contributes altogether to the account of win.

Gaining from Misfortunes: The Speculative chemistry of Development

Win over difficulty isn't only about conquering difficulties; it is an excursion of development, development, and individual speculative chemistry. Mishaps become strong open doors for self-revelation, offering people the opportunity to uncover stowed away qualities, foster strength muscles, and develop a mentality that embraces nonstop learning.

The speculative chemistry of development in the midst of difficulty includes a readiness to introspect and remove important illustrations from each mishap. Tough people view difficulties as impetuses for individual and expert turn of events, perceiving that the excursion of win is as much about the interaction for what it's worth about the objective. Every mishap turns into a pot for refining one's personality, improving abilities, and strengthening the soul.

Besides, the capacity to adjust and gain from mishaps is a sign of strong people. The speculative chemistry of development includes an outlook shift — a receptiveness to change, a readiness to embrace uneasiness, and a pledge to ceaseless improvement. Win over difficulty, in this unique situation, becomes an objective as well as an unending condition of improving as a form of oneself.

Exploring Strange Domains: The Boldness to Improve

Win over difficulty frequently expects people to explore unfamiliar regions, to get out of their usual ranges of familiarity, and to dare to improve despite difficulties. The story of flexibility is set apart by the capacity to adjust to evolving conditions, to think imaginatively, and to imagine additional opportunities where others see road obstructions.

Development with regards to misfortune includes a mentality that reexamines hindrances as any open doors for innovative critical thinking. Versatile people show the fortitude to challenge traditional standards, investigate elective ways, and trailblazer new methodologies that can prompt victory. The ability to improve isn't just a reaction to difficulty yet additionally a proactive position that enables people to shape their fates.

The boldness to enhance is intently attached to a development mentality — a conviction that capacities and knowledge can be created through commitment and difficult work. Versatile people view provokes as any open doors to extend their capacities, to explore different avenues regarding novel thoughts, and to embrace the obscure with a feeling of interest as opposed to fear. This way to deal with exploring unknown regions turns into a main thrust behind the story of win over difficulty.

From Win to Motivation: A Gradually expanding influence

The story of win over misfortune isn't bound to individual stories; it makes an expanding influence that motivates others to endure even with their difficulties. Strong people, through their activities, become encouraging signs, touching off a flash in the individuals who witness their excursions. The expanding influence of motivation rises above individual victories, cultivating an aggregate strength that penetrates networks, associations, and social orders.

Motivation frequently emerges from the accomplishment of an objective as well as from seeing the interaction — the persevering pursuit, the relentless responsibility, and the mental fortitude to face misfortune head-on. Tough people, by sharing their accounts, weaknesses, and wins, make a story that impacts others confronting comparable difficulties. This common experience turns into a wellspring of aggregate strength, supporting the conviction that victory over difficulty isn't an exception however a reachable reality.

Besides, the expanding influence of motivation reaches out past individual stories to make a social shift. Networks and social orders that celebrate versatility, recognize misfortunes as any open doors for development, and backing each other in the midst of difficulty encourage a climate where win turns into a common goal. The account of versatility changes into an aggregate story — a demonstration of the human ability to beat difficulties and arise victorious.

The Consistently Constant Soul of Win

The account of win over difficulty is an always relentless demonstration of the versatility implanted in the human soul. It is an account of boldness, tirelessness, and the faithful conviction that difficulties, regardless of how overwhelming, can be overcomed. Versatile people explore the pots of misfortune, utilizing difficulties as impetuses for development, drawing strength from emotionally supportive networks, and embracing advancement in unknown domains.

Win over difficulty isn't an objective however a ceaseless excursion — an excursion set apart by the speculative chemistry of development, the fortitude to improve, and the far reaching influence of motivation. This story, woven with strings of individual and aggregate flexibility, turns into a strong demonstration of the getting through soul of win that lives inside every individual, ready to be released when confronted with life's most imposing difficulties.

5.3. Examination of the role of community support during challenging times

Assessment of the Job of Local area Backing During Testing Times: The Bedrock of Nearby Hockey

In the multifaceted embroidery of nearby hockey, local area support arises as a basic string, winding through the difficulties and wins of players, groups, and the actual game. This assessment dives into the multi-layered job of local area support during the most testing times, delineating how the aggregate strength of a local area turns into the bedrock whereupon the building of neighborhood hockey stands.

Monetary Support: Supporting Dreams Notwithstanding Limitations

Monetary difficulties frequently cast an approaching shadow over the ways of hopeful hockey players. The expense of hardware, travel costs, interest charges, and concentrated preparing can make impressive hindrances, especially for those from monetarily distraught foundations. In these difficult times, local area support turns into an encouraging sign, offering monetary sponsorship to support the fantasies about growing players.

Nearby organizations, urban associations, and energetic local area individuals frequently rally together to make sponsorship programs, arrange pledge drives, and give monetary guide. These drives not just mitigate the monetary weight on players and their families yet in addition encourage a feeling of aggregate liability inside the local area. The interest in a player's fantasy turns into a common endeavor, supporting that, in the realm of nearby hockey, no fantasy ought to be doused because of monetary requirements.

The meaning of monetary support stretches out past individual players to the more extensive environment of neighborhood hockey associations.

Youth associations, junior groups, and local area arenas depend on monetary help to keep up with framework, coordinate competitions, and give training assets. The cooperative connection between local area support and the monetary maintainability of neighborhood hockey makes a versatile structure that endures financial difficulties and guarantees the proceeded with development of the game.

Close to home Upliftment: Exploring the Psychological Landscape

The excursion of a hockey player isn't exclusively an actual one; it crosses the complicated landscape of mental and inner difficulties. From the tensions of rivalry to the pressure of wounds and the vulnerabilities of vocation directions, players frequently wind up wrestling with the heaviness of assumptions. At these times, local area support assumes an essential part in giving profound upliftment.

Local area individuals, companions, and individual players become an encouraging group of people that reaches out past the arena. During testing times, whether it be a terrible streak, a basic physical issue, or individual mishaps, the sympathetic hug of the local area turns into a wellspring of solidarity. The consolation, understanding, and shared encounters encourage a feeling of having a place and flexibility, reminding players that they are in good company in their battles.

Mentors, tutors, and local area pioneers additionally add to the close to home prosperity of players. Their direction, persuasive discussions, and mentorship establish a sustaining climate where players can explore the psychological difficulties of the game. The aggregate capacity to understand individuals on a profound level inside the local area turns into a support against the mental cost that cutthroat games can correct, permitting players to confront difficulties with an invigorated outlook.

Expertise Improvement: Developing the Future

The improvement of hockey abilities is a persistent interaction that expects admittance to quality instructing, offices, and preparing programs. In people group where these assets might be restricted, local area support becomes instrumental in developing the up and coming age of hockey ability. Nearby legends and prepared players frequently assume the job of coaches, imparting their insight and abilities yearning for players.

Local area driven drives, for example, ability advancement camps, instructing facilities, and mentorship programs, overcome any barrier between restricted assets and the requirement for expertise upgrade. The mastery inside the local area turns into an important resource, making a recurrent cycle where experienced players add to the improvement of more youthful ability. The exchange of abilities, information, and enthusiasm inside the local area supports the game as well as guarantees its proceeded with advancement.

The job of local area support in expertise advancement reaches out to the creation and upkeep of local area arenas and hockey offices. From grassroots drives to cooperative endeavors with neighborhood specialists, networks put resources into framework that gives open spaces to practice and play. The accessibility of these offices cultivates expertise improvement as well as fills in as a bringing together power, uniting the local area around a common love for the game.

Emergency Reaction: Exploring Unforeseen Difficulties

Challenges in the realm of hockey are not restricted to the elements of the game; unanticipated emergencies, like cataclysmic events, financial slumps, or general well-being crises, can altogether affect the neighborhood hockey biological system. In the midst of emergency, local area support turns into a help, offering a fast and composed reaction to explore these unforeseen difficulties.

Local area driven aid ventures, gathering pledges crusades, and cooperative drives intend to alleviate the effect of emergencies on nearby hockey associations and players. The quick activation of assets, both monetary and material, mirrors the strength imbued locally. Whether remaking harmed offices, supporting families impacted by monetary difficulties, or tending to wellbeing and security concerns, the aggregate reaction of the local area turns into a demonstration of its fortitude.

Neighborhood organizations, which frequently assume a significant part in supporting groups or offering monetary help, may wind up confronting financial vulnerabilities during emergencies. The proportional idea of local area support is featured as the hockey local area rallies to help neighborhood organizations, guaranteeing that the harmonious relationship stays in salvageable shape. This interconnectedness turns into a critical figure enduring the hardships that compromise the security of nearby hockey.

Social Safeguarding: Supporting the Soul of the Game

Hockey isn't only a game in numerous networks; a social foundation encapsulates the soul, customs, and character of individuals. Local area support assumes an essential part in safeguarding this social importance, guaranteeing that the soul of the game is gone down through ages. Far-reaching developments, legacy festivities, and local area celebrations based on hockey become instruments for supporting the social tradition of the game.

Neighborhood organizations, craftsmen, and local area associations add to the social embroidery of hockey through sponsorships, craftsmanship establishments, and occasions that praise the game's rich history. This aggregate exertion supports that hockey isn't simply an interest yet a social resource that enhances the local area's character.

The protection of social perspectives reaches out to inclusivity and variety inside the hockey local area. Local area support turns into a main thrust in cultivating a climate where players from different foundations feel appreciated and addressed.

Drives that celebrate social variety, advance inclusivity, and teach the local area about the verifiable meaning of hockey add to an energetic and socially rich nearby hockey scene.

Local area Occasions: Cultivating Solidarity and Fellowship

The substance of nearby hockey stretches out past the limits of the arena; it flourishes in the social texture of local area occasions that unite individuals. Competitions, marches, and fan social occasions become open doors for the local area to join in festival of the game. Local area support appears in the association and cooperation in these occasions, encouraging a feeling of brotherhood and shared excitement.

Neighborhood organizations frequently assume a crucial part in supporting and putting together local area occasions, contributing monetarily as well as by making an air of celebration. The occasions become stages for organizations to draw in with the local area, reinforcing the harmonious relationship that supports nearby hockey.

Fan commitment is a urgent part of local area occasions, with allies turning into a vocal and enthusiastic expansion of the local area's help for their neighborhood groups. The aggregate cheers, serenades, and festivities during games add to the electric environment that characterizes nearby hockey. The feeling of having a place and shared pride in neighborhood groups is sustained through these common encounters, building up the reliance between the hockey local area and its allies.

Local area Backing During Testing Times: The Bedrock of Tough Social orders

In the complicated texture of human life, testing times are unavoidable — be it a worldwide emergency, a nearby disturbance, or individual battles. However, it is during these snapshots of difficulty that the genuine strength of networks arises as an encouraging sign. The pith of local area support during testing times rises above the individual, turning into an aggregate power that lightens quick difficulties as well as lays the preparation for flexibility, solidarity, and shared flourishing.

An Orchestra of Fortitude: The Aggregate Reaction to Emergency

Notwithstanding emergencies, networks organize an ensemble of fortitude, where the singular notes of sympathy, compassion, and charitableness blend to make a strong tune of help. Whether it's a catastrophic event, a wellbeing crisis, or a monetary slump, the prompt reaction of networks is portrayed by a common assurance to explore the difficulties together.

This aggregate reaction appears in different structures, from grassroots drives started by concerned residents to coordinated endeavors by local area pioneers and foundations. People rally together to give prompt guide, offering safe house, food, and daily encouragement to those impacted. Local area associations, non-benefits, and nearby organizations frequently initiate gathering pledges missions to prepare assets for everyone's benefit.

The orchestra of fortitude turns into a demonstration of the versatility imbued in the social texture, displaying that networks are more than the amount of their parts — they are a bound together power equipped for enduring tempests.

The Security Net of Consistent reassurance: Supporting Mental Prosperity

Testing times strain actual assets as well as negatively affect mental prosperity. Here, the job of local area support as a wellbeing net for profound flexibility becomes vital. In the midst of emergency, people might wrestle with dread, vulnerability, and stress. The collective hug of everyday encouragement — presented by companions, family, neighbors, and even outsiders — goes about as a medicine for the injuries of the spirit.

Local area individuals become attentive people, giving a non-critical space to people to communicate their nerves and fears. This profound fortitude cultivates a feeling of having a place and association, guaranteeing people that they are in good company to confront misfortune. Emotional wellness assets, support gatherings, and guiding administrations frequently arise inside networks to address the mental effect of testing times, building up the idea that the strength of a local area is estimated in actual assets as well as in its capacity to sustain the psychological prosperity of its individuals.

The Monetary Environment: Supporting Occupations and Organizations

Monetary slumps and emergencies can have broad outcomes, influencing jobs and organizations inside networks. In such occasions, local area support fills in as a life saver for neighborhood economies, forestalling the breakdown of organizations and defending the monetary security of people. From limited scope ventures to family-possessed organizations, the interconnected snare of financial help inside a local area turns into a vital determinant of its capacity to climate monetary tempests.

Local area individuals frequently focus on supporting nearby organizations, perceiving that the manageability of these undertakings is vital to the general prosperity of the local area. Drives, for example, "purchase nearby" crusades, local area upheld farming, and cooperative endeavors to get monetary guide for battling organizations embody the financial flexibility that arises through aggregate activity. The ethos of local area support stretches out past quick monetary help to long haul systems for manageable financial recuperation, making a strong financial environment that can endure the shocks of testing times.

Instructive Strengthening: Supporting People in the future

Testing times, particularly those influencing the school system, present huge dangers to the prosperity and future possibilities of the more youthful age. Here, people group support assumes a urgent part in guaranteeing instructive strengthening stays a need. The cooperative endeavors of guardians, teachers, local area pioneers, and nearby associations become instrumental in moderating the instructive effect of emergencies.

Networks frequently prepare assets to connect the computerized partition, guaranteeing that understudies approach important devices and advances for remote learning. Instructive help programs, mentorship drives, and local area driven coaching administrations arise to give extra help to understudies confronting difficulties. The obligation to instructive strengthening goes past emergency the board, establishing the groundwork for a versatile and knowledgeable group of people yet to come that can explore the intricacies of a consistently influencing world.

Wellbeing and Health: Fortifying the Local area Resistant Framework

Wellbeing emergencies, whether restricted or worldwide, put monstrous burden on medical services frameworks and people. In the midst of wellbeing related difficulties, local area support turns into a pivotal figure fortifying the aggregate resistant framework. From general wellbeing efforts to grassroots drives advancing solid living, networks effectively take part in encouraging a culture of prosperity that reaches out past individual wellbeing to the strength of the whole local area.

Neighborhood wellbeing facilities, public venues, and wellbeing programs assume a focal part in giving open medical care administrations. Local area individuals contribute by complying with general wellbeing rules, taking part in immunization drives, and supporting drives that focus on the wellbeing and security of all. The cooperative connection between individual prosperity and local area wellbeing becomes obvious, stressing that a local area's capacity to explore wellbeing challenges depends on the dynamic investment and backing of its individuals.

Social Conservation: Defending Character and Customs

Social strength is a characterizing part of local area support during testing times. Emergencies frequently present dangers to social personality and customs, and networks answer by effectively shielding their social legacy. Whether through craftsmanship, narrating, celebrations, or local area festivities, the protection of social practices turns into an energizing point for flexibility.

Networks join to guarantee that social organizations, legacy locales, and creative undertakings stay in one piece, perceiving the characteristic worth of social personality in the midst of emergency. Neighborhood craftsmen, social associations, and local area pioneers assume an essential part in cultivating a climate where the extravagance of social variety turns into a wellspring of solidarity and pride. Through these social protection endeavors, networks endure outer tensions as well as arise with a supported feeling of character that rises above the difficulties existing apart from everything else.

Social Inclusivity: Encouraging Solidarity In the midst of Variety

Testing times can fuel existing social abberations and imbalances. Accordingly, people group support turns into a vehicle for encouraging social inclusivity and solidarity in the midst of variety. Networks effectively work to connect separates, guaranteeing that weak populaces are not abandoned and that everybody approaches the help they need.

Inclusivity drives might incorporate local area outreach programs, mindfulness missions, and cooperation with nearby support gatherings to resolve foundational issues. The aggregate obligation to inclusivity builds up the possibility that the strength of a local area lies in its capacity to elevate every one of its individuals, paying little heed to financial foundation, nationality, or different variables. Social inclusivity turns into a foundation of strength, making a local area texture that is firmly woven with the strings of sympathy, empathy, and a common obligation to equity.

Natural Stewardship: Supporting the Biological system

Ecological difficulties, for example, cataclysmic events or environment related emergencies, highlight the interconnectedness of networks with the more extensive biological system. Here, people group support reaches out past human-driven worries to incorporate the prosperity of the climate. Limited ecological stewardship drives, for example, local area tidy up drives, tree-establishing efforts, and feasible practices, arise as vital parts of local area strength.

Networks perceive the corresponding connection between human prosperity and ecological wellbeing, understanding that an economical environment is major to their drawn out endurance. The obligation to ecological stewardship turns into a bringing together power that rises above individual interests, encouraging an awareness of certain expectations for the conservation of the regular world. Through these endeavors, networks relieve ecological difficulties as well as develop a strong relationship with the biological system they possess.

The Always Present Signal of Local area Backing

Local area support during testing times is the consistently present reference point that guides social orders through the tempests of difficulty. The diverse idea of this help — from financial strengthening and instructive flexibility to social conservation and natural stewardship — represents the all encompassing methodology networks take to explore emergencies. The aggregate reaction to provokes turns into a demonstration of the strength of human associations, the force of shared values, and the unflinching soul of versatility that characterizes networks across the globe.

As people group keep on confronting the vulnerabilities of a steadily impacting world, the story of local area support stays a tough string in the embroidery of human life. It fills in as an update that, despite misfortune, the aggregate influence of networks isn't simply a wellspring of comfort yet an extraordinary power equipped for molding a stronger, humane, and joined world.

Chapter 6

Legacy Beyond the Ice

Inheritance Past the Ice

Inheritance Past the Ice is a thorough investigation of the diverse effect of ice sports on people, networks, and the world overall. This top to bottom story looks to unwind the layers of importance implanted in the heritages made by competitors, the extraordinary force of sports, and the enduring engraving left on social orders. As we set out on this excursion, we dig into the complicated snare of stories that reach out a long ways past the arena, enlightening the getting through impact of ice sports on culture, personality, and human associations.

At the core of Inheritance Past the Ice are the competitors who rise above their jobs as rivals to become social symbols and envoys for change. Their accounts, frequently established in humble starting points, unfurl as demonstrations of the groundbreaking force of devotion and flexibility. From the early morning rehearses on frozen lakes to the worldwide phases of rivalry, these competitors encapsulate the upsides of discipline, diligence, and energy that stretch out a long ways past the limits of the ice.

The narrative unfurls against the scenery of the rich history and social meaning of ice sports. From the great starting points of figure skating to the adrenaline-siphoning power of ice hockey, each discipline adds to the assorted woven artwork of the donning scene. Heritage Past the Ice honors the trailblazers who laid the foundation for these games, enlightening the development of methods, styles, and the social subtleties that make each discipline an extraordinary articulation of human physicality.

As the story unfurls, we witness the significant effect of ice sports on networks all over the planet. Nearby arenas become favorable places for ability, encouraging a feeling of kinship and divided character between yearning competitors. Heritage Past the Ice investigates the grassroots drives that engage youthful skaters, making pathways for ability to bloom and moving the up and coming age of champions. The arena, when a simple battleground, changes into a space where dreams are sustained and desires take off.

Past the individual accomplishments of competitors, Inheritance Past the Ice digs into the social and social elements of ice sports. The narrative analyzes how these games act as stages for social trade, separating boundaries and encouraging comprehension among different networks. Ice sports become a widespread language that rises above borders, joining people from various foundations in a common quest for greatness and sportsmanship.

The groundbreaking force of ice sports is additionally clear in the tales of competitors who influence their foundation to drive positive change. Inheritance Past the Ice features occasions where competitors become advocates for civil rights, natural maintainability, and inclusivity. Through meetings and in the background film, the narrative investigates the manners by which these competitors take advantage of their leverage to resolve squeezing worldwide issues, broadening their heritages past the limits of the brandishing field.

The effect of ice sports on self-improvement is a repetitive subject in Heritage Past the Ice. The discipline expected for authority of these games imparts significant fundamental abilities, for example, using time productively, objective setting, and collaboration. Through interviews with competitors, mentors, and sports analysts, the narrative digs into the mental and close to home parts of the excursion, revealing insight into the psychological backbone expected to explore the ups and downs of serious games.

Inheritance Past the Ice likewise looks at the advantageous connection among competitors and their networks. The emotionally supportive networks that arise around these people, from loved ones to nearby fan bases, assume an essential part in molding the story of progress. The narrative catches the close to home reverberation of crucial minutes, from the cheerful festivals of triumphs to the aggregate strength notwithstanding misfortunes. These accounts highlight the shared idea of sports and the enduring bonds manufactured among competitors and the people who rally behind them.

Inheritance Past the Ice is a convincing odyssey that rises above the limits of conventional games narratives. It winds around together the individual accounts of competitors, the social meaning of ice sports, and the cultural effect of these disciplines. Through a nuanced investigation of the inheritances made both on and off the ice, the narrative welcomes watchers to consider the getting through impact of sports on people, networks, and the more extensive human experience.

6.1. Discussion on the lasting impact local legends have on their communities Conversation on the Enduring Effect Nearby Legends Have on Their People group

The idea of neighborhood legends holds a novel and strong spot in the shared perspective of networks. These figures, frequently established in the domains of sports, expressions, or community administration, become residing exemplifications of the qualities, yearnings, and character of the spots they call home. In this broad conversation, we investigate the significant and enduring effect nearby legends have on their networks, digging into the manners by which these figures shape the story, rouse people in the future, and cultivate a feeling of having a place.

Nearby legends, whether rising up out of the universe of sports, expressions, or local area administration, become social standards that characterize the substance of a local area. Their effect stretches out past individual accomplishments, meshing into the actual texture of the aggregate character. These figures frequently typify the qualities that resound with the local area — values like versatility, diligence, and a pledge to greatness. The tales of neighborhood legends become stories of shared pride, filling in as a wellspring of motivation that joins local area individuals under a typical pennant.

In the domain of sports, nearby legends take on an especially famous status. Whether it's the star quarterback who drove the secondary school football crew to triumph or the ball wonder who arose out of humble starting points to arrive at the expert associations, these competitors become inseparable from the soul of their networks. Their accomplishments on the field rise above simple athletic ability; they become images of old neighborhood pride and strength, revitalizing focuses for local area attachment.

One of the vital parts of the enduring effect of nearby legends is their capacity to rouse people in the future. As youthful hopeful people observer the victories and battles of these nearby symbols, they find engaging good examples who have strolled similar roads and confronted comparable difficulties. The accounts of neighborhood legends become inspirational stories, delineating that significance can rise out of even the most improbable conditions. This motivation frequently reaches out past the particular main subject area, affecting youthful personalities to seek after their interests, whether in sports, scholastics, or human expression.

The association between neighborhood legends and local area advancement is complex and cooperative. These figures frequently act as impetuses for positive change, utilizing their impact to resolve social issues, support neighborhood drives, and add to the general prosperity of their networks. The enduring effect isn't bound to the greatness days of a competitor's prime or a craftsman's pinnacle; it stretches out into the continuous endeavors of these nearby legends to offer in return and have a significant effect where they are established.

In looking at the enduring effect of nearby legends, it's vital to perceive the job of narrating. The accounts woven around these figures, whether through nearby media, oral practices, or local area festivities, shape the view of their heritage. The tales told about nearby legends add to the production of a common social memory, protecting the substance of their commitments for people in the future. The most common way of narrating turns into a method for communicating values, ingraining a feeling of progression, and supporting the ties that tight spot a local area together.

Nearby legends frequently act as extension developers, interfacing various ages inside a local area. The more seasoned individuals, who saw the ascent of these figures, track down a wellspring of sentimentality and an association with their own past. At the same time, the more youthful age finds a connection to the local area's set of experiences and legacy through the stories of these neighborhood symbols. This intergenerational association cultivates a feeling of coherence and shared character, supporting that the local area is essential for a bigger, continuous story.

Additionally, the effect of neighborhood legends isn't restricted to geographic limits; it resounds in the hearts and psyches of people who might have moved away yet at the same time convey the soul of their old neighborhood legends with them. This diasporic impact effectively interfaces far off local area individuals, making a common character that rises above actual space. The persevering through effect of neighborhood legends turns into a wellspring of association and pride for people who might end up in various corners of the world.

With regards to expressions and culture, nearby legends assume a significant part in molding the imaginative personality of a local area. Whether it's a commended performer, a prestigious painter, or a respected essayist, these social symbols add to the enhancement of the neighborhood creative scene. Their work turns into an impression of the local area's spirit, catching its subtleties, battles, and wins. The social heritage left by these craftsmen turns into a wellspring of motivation for hopeful makers and a demonstration of the dynamic quality of the neighborhood imaginative scene.

Nearby legends likewise assume an essential part in encouraging a feeling of local area pride and union. Their accomplishments, whether on the games field or the imaginative stage, make snapshots of shared festival that rise above friendly, financial, and social partitions.

The solidarity manufactured in celebrating neighborhood legends turns into an establishment for more extensive local area commitment and joint effort. It gives a shared view where people from different foundations can meet up to celebrate shared accomplishments and values.

A fascinating component of the effect of nearby legends is their part in forming the impression of a local area from an outer stance. These figures frequently become the essence of the places where they grew up, adding to the local area's standing on a provincial, public, or even global scale. The accomplishments and character of neighborhood legends become interlaced with the picture of the local area itself, affecting the way things are seen by those external its lines.

The effect of nearby legends isn't safe to the progression of time. As people group advance, the accounts around these figures might go through reevaluation or change. In any case, the persevering through parts of their effect — the motivation they give, the feeling of local area they encourage, and the social heritage they abandon — keep on resounding through the changing tides of cultural turn of events. Neighborhood legends, in this sense, become immortal images that associate the past, present, and eventual fate of a local area.

The conversation on the enduring effect neighborhood legends have on their networks is a nuanced investigation of the multi-layered manners by which these figures shape, move, and add to the aggregate personality of a region. Whether in the domain of sports, expressions, or municipal administration, nearby legends make a permanent imprint that reaches out a long ways past individual accomplishments. They become mainstays of motivation, impetuses for positive change, and living encapsulations of the qualities that characterize their networks. The persevering through tradition of nearby legends fills in as a demonstration of the flexibility, imagination, and interconnectedness of networks, delineating that significance can rise out of the most unforeseen corners of our common human experience.

6.2. Exploration of post-playing careers, coaching, and mentorship by these players

Investigation of Post-Playing Professions, Instructing, and Mentorship by Competitors

The excursion of a competitor reaches out a long ways past the years spent contending on the field. While the spotlight frequently centers around their exhibitions during their playing vocations, what unfolds after the last whistle or the last game is similarly entrancing. This investigation digs into the post-playing professions of competitors, with a specific accentuation on their jobs as mentors and guides. It unwinds the tales of people who progress from being headliners to becoming persuasive figures directing the future, forming the scene of sports long after they've hung up their pullovers.

One noticeable road for competitors in their post-playing vocations is training. The change from player to mentor is a characteristic development for some who try to channel their skill and enthusiasm for the game into sustaining the gifts of yearning competitors.

Instructing permits these people to share the abundance of information they've gathered over long stretches of preparing and contest. The effect of an accomplished the mentor ups and downs of the game firsthand is unfathomable, as they bring an interesting point of view and a sympathetic comprehension of the difficulties looked by those they coach.

The choice to turn into a mentor is much of the time driven by a firmly established want to reward the game that has formed a competitor's life. It addresses a continuation of their excursion inside the domain of sports, yet from an alternate vantage point. As mentors, previous competitors become engineers of ability advancement, molding the abilities, character, and outlook of the future. This change from the battleground to the sidelines isn't simply a lifelong decision; it is a significant obligation to passing on the light of information and imparting an affection for the game in others.

Mentorship is an equal component of the post-playing vocations of competitors, interweaving with instructing to make a comprehensive way to deal with player improvement. Past the specialized parts of the game, mentorship includes granting life illustrations, ingraining values, and giving direction on exploring the difficulties that reach out past the games field. Competitors turned-coaches become more than educators; they become associates, wellsprings of motivation, and mainstays of help for those under the care of them.

The guide mentee relationship is many times portrayed by an interesting bond fashioned through shared encounters. Previous competitors figure out the tensions, wins, and mishaps that accompany chasing after a lifelong in sports. This common foundation makes a degree of understanding and trust that is significant in the mentorship dynamic. Coaches draw on their own excursions to offer guidance, support, and a feeling of point of view to the people who admire them, making a cooperative relationship that rises above the simply proficient.

The effect of competitor mentors and tutors stretches out past the improvement of specialized abilities. They assume a pivotal part in molding the person and upsides of the competitors they guide. The accentuation on discipline, cooperation, flexibility, and sportsmanship turns into a foundation of their mentorship reasoning. By conferring these characteristics, competitor mentors and tutors contribute not exclusively to the development of talented competitors yet in addition to the advancement of balanced people who convey these qualities into different parts of their lives.

In investigating the post-playing professions of competitors, it's fundamental to perceive the expanding influence of their impact. As mentors and guides, they become modelers of a social inheritance inside sports associations and networks. The standards they impart establish a positive and supporting climate that stretches out a long ways past the prompt effect on individual competitors. The way of life of sports associations molded by previous players is much of the time portrayed by a pledge to greatness, a solid feeling of kinship, and an emphasis on comprehensive competitor improvement.

The progress to instructing and mentorship isn't without its difficulties. Previous competitors should explore the shift from being forced to bear training to accepting the job of the mentor or coach. This progress includes leveling up new abilities, like correspondence, initiative, and the capacity to fit training ways to deal with the assorted requirements of competitors. It likewise requires a change in context, as mentors and tutors should now zero in on the aggregate outcome of their group or mentees as opposed to individual achievements.

In spite of the difficulties, the change to training and mentorship offers competitors a chance for individual and expert development. It gives a stage to them to keep making a significant commitment to the games world while likewise developing as pioneers and forces to be reckoned with. The bits of knowledge acquired from their own processes add a layer of credibility to their training and tutoring styles, encouraging associations with competitors in light of shared encounters and common comprehension.

The effect of competitor mentors and guides isn't restricted to the domain of serious games. Their impact stretches out into more extensive cultural settings, where the qualities they impart rise above the limits of the battleground. Competitors who change to training and mentorship positions become good examples for trying people, displaying that achievement isn't bound to a limited time of athletic rivalry yet can be a long lasting excursion of constant development and commitment.

Past the prompt circle of sports, the post-playing vocations of competitors likewise include jobs as representatives, supporters, and local area pioneers. Numerous previous competitors influence their foundation to support social causes, bring issues to light about significant issues, and add to positive change in their networks. Their impact stretches out past the bounds of the games field, showing the potential for competitors to be impetuses for more extensive cultural effect.

The idea of competitors as local area pioneers is especially obvious in occurrences where previous players effectively take part in altruism, local area administration, and youth improvement drives. Perceiving the effect they can have on the existences of others, these people utilize their assets and impact to make programs that enable youngsters, advance instruction, and address cultural difficulties. The post-playing professions of competitors hence become a demonstration of the extraordinary force of sports as a power for positive change.

Post-playing Vocations, Training, and Mentorship: Molding Inheritances Past the Field

The finish of a competitor's playing vocation doesn't stamp the finish of their excursion in the realm of sports; rather, it frequently flags the start of another part — one characterized by training, mentorship, and a significant obligation to forming the fate of the game. This change from the job of a player to that of a mentor or tutor is a basic crossroads in the existence of a competitor, addressing an individual development as well as an enduring commitment to the world they have committed their lives to.

Training arises as a characteristic pathway for the vast majority resigned competitors, giving a road to channel their abundance of involvement, information, and enthusiasm for the game into sustaining the gifts of the future. The training job is multi-layered, requiring specialized mastery as well as compelling correspondence, initiative, and a sharp comprehension of the mental parts of execution. Competitor mentors have an exceptional benefit — they bring a personal information on the game, having encountered its complexities, tensions, and wins firsthand.

The choice to set out on a training vocation is in many cases filled by a longing to reward the game that has formed a competitor's character. It's a significant obligation to cultivating ability improvement and passing on the light of information. Competitor mentors become planners of athletic abilities as well as of character, imparting values like discipline, cooperation, versatility, and sportsmanship. The effect of a survived the mentor ups and downs of the game goes past the specialized viewpoints; it reaches out into the domain of mentorship, where competitors track down direction in their game as well as throughout everyday life.

Mentorship, related to training, addresses a more profound layer of the competitor's post-playing profession. The guide mentee relationship is described by a special bond produced through shared encounters. Previous competitors who progress to mentorship jobs draw on their own excursions to offer exhortation, support, and a feeling of viewpoint. The coach turns out to be in excess of an educator; they become a comrade, a wellspring of motivation, and an aide through the difficulties that reach out past the games field. This double job as a mentor and coach makes an all encompassing way to deal with player improvement, tending to the specialized abilities expected for progress as well as the self-awareness and strength expected to explore the intricacies of life.

The effect of competitor mentors and coaches is significant and sweeping. Past the prompt improvement of individual competitors, they assume a pivotal part in molding the way of life of sports associations and networks. The standards they ingrain establish a positive and sustaining climate, encouraging a promise to greatness, a solid feeling of kinship, and an emphasis on comprehensive competitor improvement. This social heritage reaches out past the prompt effect on players; it turns into an enduring commitment that shapes the ethos of the whole games local area.

The change from player to mentor or guide isn't without its difficulties. Previous competitors should explore the shift from being the one getting instructing to taking on the obligation of directing others. This progress includes leveling up new abilities, adjusting instructing ways to deal with different individual necessities, and cultivating a group situated mentality. Competitor mentors and tutors should likewise battle with the change in context — from zeroing in on individual achievements to focusing on the aggregate progress of their group or mentees. A change requires a mix of lowliness, versatility, and a certifiable obligation to the development of those under their direction.

In spite of the difficulties, the change to training and mentorship offers competitors a stage for individual and expert development. It addresses a chance to keep making a significant commitment to the games world while developing as pioneers and powerhouses. The bits of knowledge acquired from their own processes add a layer of realness to their training and tutoring styles, cultivating associations with competitors in light of shared encounters and common comprehension. The mentorship job, specifically, permits previous competitors to pass on specialized abilities as well as the elusive characteristics that characterize fruitful people both on and off the field.

The effect of competitor mentors and coaches isn't bound to the domain of serious games. Their impact stretches out into more extensive cultural settings, where the qualities they ingrain rise above the limits of the battleground. Competitors who change to instructing and mentorship positions become good examples for trying people, displaying that achievement isn't bound to a limited time of athletic rivalry however can be a deep rooted excursion of persistent development and commitment.

Past instructing and mentorship, the post-playing vocations of competitors likewise include jobs as ministers, promoters, and local area pioneers. Numerous previous competitors influence their foundation to support social causes, bring issues to light about significant issues, and add to positive change in their networks. Their impact stretches out past the limits of the games field, delineating the potential for competitors to be impetuses for more extensive cultural effect.

The idea of competitors as local area pioneers is especially obvious in cases where previous players effectively participate in charity, local area administration, and youth advancement drives. Perceiving the effect they can have on the existences of others, these people utilize their assets and impact to make programs that engage youngsters, advance schooling, and address cultural difficulties. The post-playing professions of competitors subsequently become a demonstration of the extraordinary force of sports as a power for positive change.

The investigation of post-playing vocations, instructing, and mentorship by competitors uncovers a dynamic and multi-layered scene. The progress from headliner to compelling mentor or guide is an excursion set apart by a profound obligation to the game, a longing to offer in return, and an acknowledgment of the extraordinary force of shared encounters. Competitors who embrace instructing and mentorship jobs become engineers of ability improvement, instillers of values, and supporters of a positive games culture. Past the bounds of the battleground, their impact stretches out into cultural domains, where they become envoys for change, advocates for social causes, and pioneers in their networks. The post-playing professions of competitors, in this broad sense, represent that their effect isn't bound to snapshots of athletic greatness yet resounds as a long lasting tradition of commitment and impact.

6.3. Analysis of the lasting legacy and inspiration they provide to aspiring young players

Investigation of the Enduring Inheritance and Motivation Given by Competitors to Hopeful Youthful Players

The effect of competitors reaches out past the limits of the battleground; it rises above the snapshots of triumph or rout and stretches out into the hearts and brains of hopeful youthful players. The enduring heritage made by competitors, especially the people who progress to instructing and mentorship jobs, turns into a wellspring of motivation that shapes the fate of sports. In this examination, we dig into the significant and persevering through impact that these competitors apply on the future, looking at the manners by which their heritage turns into a main impetus for hopeful youthful players.

One of the most unmistakable parts of the enduring inheritance left by competitors is the specialized and strategic information they give yearning for players. Competitor mentors bring an abundance of involvement and skill gained over long periods of thorough preparation and contest. This information is priceless in molding the abilities and comprehension of the game for youthful competitors. The subtleties of system, the complexities of procedure, and the psychological parts of execution are complicatedly woven into the texture of instructing and mentorship. Hopeful players benefit from the hypothetical angles as well as from the commonsense bits of knowledge acquired through the mentorship of the individuals who have explored similar difficulties.

Past the details, the tradition of competitors impacts the mentality and character of yearning players. The qualities imparted by competitor mentors and coaches reach out a long ways past the battleground. Ideas like discipline, strength, cooperation, and sportsmanship become indispensable parts of the heritage they pass on. These qualities, fashioned through the pot of athletic contest, act as core values for youthful players as they explore the intricacies of the two games and life. The persevering through influence lies in the change of talented competitors as well as balanced people who convey these qualities into different features of their lives.

The individual stories and excursions of competitors turned-mentors become accounts of motivation for hopeful youthful players. The stories of win over affliction, the versatility despite misfortunes, and the commitment to constant improvement reverberate profoundly with the people who fantasy about emulating their example. Competitors who change to instructing jobs carry genuineness to their accounts, permitting hopeful players to see past the glamour of achievement and value the human part of the excursion. These accounts become encouraging signs, showing that significance is many times produced in the pot of difficulties and mishaps.

The mentorship given by competitors fills in as a strong inspiration for youthful players. The one-on-one direction, exhortation, and consolation establish a customized and steady climate that cultivates development and improvement. The tutor mentee relationship rises above the simply specialized parts of the game; it turns into a wellspring of everyday encouragement, a sounding board for yearnings and concerns, and an organization chasing greatness. Hopeful players track down mentors as well as coaches who really care about their comprehensive turn of events, both as competitors and people.

The appeal of competitor mentors and guides contributes essentially to the enduring heritage they make. As people who have strolled similar way, confronted comparative difficulties, and remained in similar shoes, these competitors become engaging figures for trying players. The nearness of involvement makes a feeling of association and understanding that rises above the common mentor player relationship. This appeal is a critical calculate separating obstructions and rousing trust in youthful players, as they see substantial confirmation that achievement is feasible with devotion and difficult work.

The effect of competitor mentors and coaches stretches out past the quick specialized and self-improvement of trying players; it turns into an impetus for social change inside sports associations and networks. The positive qualities, hard working attitude, and obligation to greatness developed by these competitors shape the ethos of the groups and clubs they are related with. The way of life of progress and shared regard turns into a sign of the inheritance they abandon, impacting individual players as well as the more extensive games local area. This social shift adds to the formation of conditions where youthful players flourish as competitors as well as mindful and compassionate people.

The awareness of certain expectations that competitor mentors feel towards their mentees further highlights the enduring inheritance they plan to make. Past the craving for individual achievement, these competitors are driven by a pledge to add to the improvement of the future. This feeling of obligation turns into a directing power in their training and mentorship jobs, as they effectively look to establish good and enabling conditions for youthful players. The persevering through influence lies not just in the specialized and strategic perspectives conferred yet in addition in the mentorship that shape the person and benefits of trying competitors.

The openness of competitor mentors and guides in the post-playing stage is a huge calculate the enduring heritage they make. Not at all like far off calculates whose impact might be bound to the feature reels, these competitors are effectively partici-pated in the everyday advancement of youthful players. The nearness considers a more customized and involved way to deal with instructing and mentorship. Hopeful players have direct admittance to the abundance of information and experience these competitors bring, encouraging a dynamic and responsive learning climate that speeds up their development.

The getting through effect of competitor mentors and coaches additionally lies in the gradually expanding influence they make inside networks. As the competitors turned-mentors effectively draw in with neighborhood sports projects, schools, and youth improvement drives, their impact reaches out a long ways past the prompt circle of cutthroat games. The positive qualities, hard working attitude, and feeling of local area imparted by these competitors become a wellspring of motivation for youthful people in the more extensive local area. The openness and association of competitor mentors in local area drives add to the production of positive good examples for trying players, outlining that outcome in sports is entwined with a promise to local area prosperity.

The motivation given by competitor mentors and tutors isn't restricted to the specialized and strategic parts of the game. It reaches out into cultivating an adoration for the game and a long lasting enthusiasm for active work. The energy and devotion these competitors bring to their training jobs make an irresistible environment that reverberates with youthful players. The delight of playing, the excitement of rivalry, and the fellowship produced on the field become basic parts of the heritage these com-petitors abandon. Hopeful players foster their abilities as well as develop a certifiable and persevering through adoration for the game.

The enduring heritage and motivation left by competitors stretch out a long ways past the limits of the battleground, winding around a story of effect that rises above triumphs and losses. These competitors, especially the people who change into train-ing and mentorship jobs, engrave their impact on the hearts and brains of hopeful youthful players, forming the eventual fate of sports with a profundity that goes past specialized abilities. In this examination, we investigate the significant and getting through nature of this heritage, looking at the manners by which it turns into a main thrust for motivation, inspiration, and self-awareness for the future.

One of the most unmistakable parts of the enduring inheritance left by competitors is the specialized and key information they grant striving for players. Competitors turned-mentors bring an abundance of involvement, offering experiences into the complexities of the game that must be acquired through long stretches of thorough preparation and rivalry. This information, shared through training and mentorship, turns into a reference point for youthful competitors trying to improve their abilities and comprehension of the game. The strategic subtleties, key bits of knowledge, and mental mettle developed by these competitors act as a guide for hopeful players exploring their own excursions in the realm of sports.

Past the details, the tradition of competitors significantly impacts the mentality and character of trying players. The qualities imparted by competitor mentors reach out past the domain of sports, becoming necessary parts of the individual and moral advancement of youthful competitors. Ideas like discipline, strength, cooperation, and sportsmanship become core values that stretch out into different aspects of their lives. The getting through influence lies in the change of talented competitors as well as balanced people who convey these qualities into their connections, training, and future professions.

The individual stories and excursions of competitors turned-mentors become accounts of motivation for hopeful youthful players. The stories of win over difficulty, the versatility notwithstanding misfortunes, and the devotion to nonstop improvement reverberate profoundly with the people who fantasy about emulating their example. Competitors who progress to instructing jobs carry legitimacy to their accounts, permitting hopeful players to see past the sparkling snapshots of achievement and value the human part of the excursion. These accounts become strong inspirations, delineating that significance is many times manufactured in the cauldron of difficulties and misfortunes.

The mentorship given by competitors fills in as a powerful wellspring of motivation for youthful players. The one-on-one direction, exhortation, and consolation establish a customized and steady climate that cultivates athletic development as well as self-awareness. The tutor mentee relationship rises above the specialized parts of the game; it turns into a wellspring of consistent encouragement, a sounding board for yearnings and concerns, and an organization chasing greatness. Hopeful players track down mentors as well as guides who really care about their all encompassing turn of events, both as competitors and people.

The appeal of competitor mentors and tutors is a significant consider the enduring heritage they make. As people who have strolled similar way, confronted comparative difficulties, and remained in similar shoes, these competitors become engaging figures for yearning players. The vicinity of involvement makes a feeling of association and understanding that rises above the normal mentor player relationship. This appeal is instrumental in breaking down boundaries and motivating trust in youthful players, as they see substantial proof that achievement is feasible with commitment and difficult work.

The effect of competitor mentors and tutors reaches out past the quick specialized and self-awareness of trying players; it turns into an impetus for social change inside sports associations and networks. The positive qualities, hard working attitude, and obligation to greatness developed by these competitors shape the ethos of the groups and clubs they are related with. The way of life of progress and shared regard turns into a sign of the inheritance they abandon, impacting individual players as well as the more extensive games local area. This social shift adds to the making of conditions where youthful players flourish as competitors as well as mindful and sympathetic people.

The awareness of others' expectations that competitor mentors feel toward their mentees further highlights the enduring inheritance they intend to make. Past the craving for individual achievement, these competitors are driven by a guarantee to add to the improvement of the future. This feeling of obligation turns into a directing power in their training and mentorship jobs, as they effectively look to establish good and enabling conditions for youthful players. The getting through influence lies not just in the specialized and strategic perspectives conferred yet in addition in the mentorship that shape the person and benefits of trying competitors.

The openness of competitor mentors and tutors in the post-playing stage is a huge consider the enduring heritage they make. Not at all like far off calculates whose impact might be restricted to the feature reels, these competitors are effectively taken part in the everyday improvement of youthful players. The vicinity considers a more customized and involved way to deal with instructing and mentorship. Hopeful players have direct admittance to the abundance of information and experience these competitors bring, cultivating a dynamic and responsive learning climate that speeds up their development.

The getting through effect of competitor mentors and tutors likewise lies in the far reaching influence they make inside networks. As the competitors turned-mentors effectively draw in with neighborhood sports projects, schools, and youth advancement drives, their impact reaches out a long ways past the prompt circle of serious games. The positive qualities, hard working attitude, and feeling of local area imparted by these competitors become a wellspring of motivation for youthful people in the more extensive local area. The openness and inclusion of competitor mentors in local area drives add to the production of positive good examples for yearning players, outlining that outcome in sports is entwined with a promise to local area prosperity.

The motivation given by competitor mentors and guides isn't restricted to the specialized and strategic parts of the game. It reaches out into cultivating an adoration for the game and a long lasting enthusiasm for actual work. The excitement and devotion these competitors bring to their instructing jobs make an irresistible climate that resounds with youthful players. The delight of playing, the excitement of contest, and the fellowship produced on the field become basic parts of the inheritance these competitors abandon. Hopeful players foster their abilities as well as develop a veritable and persevering through adoration for the game.

The investigation of the enduring inheritance and motivation given by competitors to hopeful youthful players uncovers a rich embroidery of impact that reaches out a long ways past the domains of specialized instructing. Competitor mentors and guides become engineers of both athletic and self-awareness, molding the person, values, and outlook of the future. The persevering through influence lies in the appeal, validness, and openness of these competitors, making a culture of progress and positive qualities inside sports associations and networks. The motivation given by these competitors turns into an impetus for social change, local area commitment, and the comprehensive improvement of hopeful players who lead of their inheritance into what's in store.

Chapter 7

Contextual investigations

Contextual investigations assume a urgent part in different fields, giving a top to bottom investigation of explicit occurrences or situations to extricate significant bits of knowledge, examples, and arrangements. Whether applied in business, schooling, brain science, or examination, contextual investigations offer a thorough comprehension of true circumstances, empowering a more profound examination of the elements at play. In this investigation of contextual analyses, we dig into their importance, systems, and the assorted settings where they are utilized.

At its center, a contextual investigation is a nitty gritty assessment of a specific subject, frequently centered around a solitary individual, gathering, occasion, or peculiarity. The essential goal is to acquire a nuanced comprehension of the subject and uncover bits of knowledge that probably won't be clear through more extensive factual or hypothetical investigations. Contextual investigations are described by their profundity and setting explicit nature, permitting scientists and professionals to investigate the complexities of a circumstance and make significant inferences.

The meaning of contextual analyses lies in their capacity to overcome any issues among hypothesis and practice. While speculations give a structure to understanding peculiarities, contextual analyses rejuvenate these hypotheses by outlining how they work in certifiable settings. This applied methodology approves or refine hypothetical ideas, making them more material and applicable. Moreover, contextual investigations add to the advancement of new hypotheses by uncovering examples, connections, and elements that probably won't be quickly clear through other exploration strategies.

One critical component in the development of a contextual analysis is the determination of a subject that is both pertinent to the exploration question and offers a rich wellspring of data. The subject can go from people or gatherings to associations, occasions, or cycles. The scientist intends to pick a case that not just lines up with the targets of the concentrate yet additionally gives an exhaustive perspective on the peculiarity being scrutinized.

The strategy utilized on the off chance that reviews differs relying upon the exploration objectives and the idea of the subject. Notwithstanding, there are normal components that describe the interaction. Information assortment frequently includes a blend of strategies like meetings, perceptions, report examination, and, at times, studies. The triangulation of information from different sources improves the legitimacy and unwavering quality of the discoveries. Specialists additionally give close consideration to the setting in which the case is arranged, taking into account factors like time, spot, and social elements.

The top to bottom nature of contextual investigations considers a comprehensive assessment of the subject, catching the detectable ways of behaving as well as the hidden inspirations, perspectives, and logical impacts. This profundity is especially significant in understanding complex peculiarities where numerous factors communicate. For instance, a contextual investigation on the progress of a specific business could investigate not exclusively its monetary procedures yet in addition its hierarchical culture, authority style, and reaction to showcase elements.

In business and the executives, contextual analyses are broadly used for their capacity to give experiences into key navigation, hierarchical way of behaving, and industry elements. For example, a contextual investigation on the circle back of a weak organization could break down the initiative choices, functional changes, and outside factors that added to its recuperation. The extravagance of data acquired from such examinations can offer significant examples for professionals and act as instructive apparatuses in scholarly settings.

In the domain of training, contextual analyses are every now and again utilized to improve growth opportunities. Teachers utilize certifiable guides to represent hypothetical ideas, permitting understudies to apply their insight to pragmatic circumstances.

For example, a contextual investigation on a verifiable occasion could provoke understudies to dissect the political, social, and monetary elements that molded the result, encouraging decisive reasoning and logical abilities.

Brain research uses contextual analyses to dig into the intricacies of individual way of behaving, mental cycles, and mental problems. In clinical brain science, for instance, contextual investigations give a nitty gritty assessment of a patient's experience, side effects, and treatment, offering bits of knowledge into the viability of helpful methodologies. These examinations add to the advancement of proof based rehearses and advise the more extensive field regarding brain science.

In the field of medication, contextual analyses assume a fundamental part in propelling comprehension and treatment techniques. Clinical contextual investigations, which detail the analysis, therapy, and results of individual patients, contribute significant data to clinical writing. They act as an establishment for proof based medication, illuminating medical care experts about prescribed procedures in different clinical situations. Furthermore, epidemiological contextual analyses are significant for understanding the spread of sicknesses, recognizing risk factors, and illuminating general wellbeing mediations.

Sociologies, including humanism and humanities, influence contextual analyses to investigate social peculiarities, cultural designs, and individual encounters. Ethnographic contextual analyses, for example, submerge scientists in the regular routines of networks, offering a nuanced comprehension of their traditions, values, and social elements. These examinations add to diverse comprehension and challenge assumptions by giving setting rich experiences.

Natural sciences use contextual investigations to analyze biological frameworks, preservation endeavors, and the effect of human exercises on the climate. A contextual investigation on a specific environment could examine the exchange between biodiversity, environmental change, and preservation strategies. The discoveries can illuminate ecological administration systems and add to worldwide discussions on supportability.

Research in political theory frequently utilizes contextual analyses to examine explicit occasions, approaches, or political frameworks. These investigations can give a nitty gritty assessment of the variables impacting political choices, the effect of strategies on society, or the elements of global relations. By digging into the particulars of a case, political researchers can draw more extensive ramifications and add to hypothetical structures inside the discipline.

In innovation and advancement, contextual analyses are important for figuring out the turn of events and reception of new advances. For instance, a contextual investigation on the presentation of a momentous innovation in a particular industry could investigate the difficulties confronted, the procedures utilized, and the general effect on the area. This information is critical for illuminating future innovative headways and reception systems.

While contextual investigations offer an abundance of advantages, they are not without challenges. The potential for predisposition, restricted generalizability, and the emotional idea of understanding are innate dangers. Specialists should explore these difficulties by utilizing thorough strategies, guaranteeing straightforwardness in information assortment and examination, and recognizing the impediments of their discoveries. Notwithstanding these difficulties, the qualities of contextual investigations in giving profundity, setting, and certifiable pertinence make them an important device across different disciplines.

Contextual investigations act as a strong strategic instrument across different disciplines, giving a nuanced comprehension of explicit occurrences or peculiarities. Their top to bottom investigation of certifiable circumstances offers significant bits of knowledge, examples, and arrangements that add to hypothetical systems, proof based rehearses, and informed navigation. From business and training to brain research, medication, and the sociologies, contextual analyses assume a urgent part in propelling information, cultivating decisive reasoning, and overcoming any issues among hypothesis and practice. As scientists and professionals keep on tackling the capability of contextual investigations, their persevering through significance in producing setting explicit information stays a foundation of observational request.

7.1. In-depth studies of specific local legends and their contributions

Top to bottom Investigations of Explicit Nearby Legends and Their Commitments

Nearby legends, frequently worshipped figures inside their networks, convey a significant effect that reaches out past the prompt bounds of their accomplishments. These figures, whether in the domain of sports, culture, or local area authority, become images of motivation, strength, and the epitome of shared values. In this investigation, we dive into the meaning of directing top to bottom investigations of explicit nearby legends, unwinding their accounts, commitments, and the persevering through heritages they leave inside the embroidery of their networks.

One of the essential inspirations for leading top to bottom investigations of nearby legends lies in the rich woven artwork of accounts they bring to their particular networks. These people, frequently molded by the interesting setting of their regions, become living storehouses of history, culture, and local area ethos. By diving into their accounts, scientists can uncover the multifaceted strings that weave the texture of the local area, understanding the elements that have shaped these considers along with nearby legends. This story investigation goes past measurable information, giving a subjective comprehension of the human encounters, difficulties, and wins that characterize these people.

Neighborhood legends are results of their networks as well as supporters of the aggregate character of the districts they address. Inside and out examinations permit analysts to investigate the cooperative connection between these figures and their networks, revealing insight into how their commitments have molded nearby culture, values, and desires.

Whether through imaginative undertakings, athletic accomplishments, or local area administration, nearby legends become social draftsmen, affecting the manner in which networks see themselves and their common personality. Understanding these elements is critical for protecting and improving the social legacy of a local area.

In the domain of sports, nearby legends frequently arise as images of athletic ability, devotion, and the soul of contest. Top to bottom investigations of these competitors go past the scores and measurements, revealing the individual stories, forfeits, and preparing regimens that have pushed them to famous status inside their networks. By breaking down their excursion from hopeful competitors to neighborhood legends, analysts can recognize examples of progress, versatility despite affliction, and the effect of mentorship on the improvement of wearing greatness.

Besides, the investigation of nearby legends in sports offers bits of knowledge into the job of games as a vehicle for local area pride and union. Through top to bottom investigations, analysts can analyze how these figures act as binding together images, mobilizing focuses for local area backing, and wellsprings of motivation for the more youthful age. This examination goes past the singular competitor's accomplishments, stretching out to the more extensive ramifications for local area wellbeing, commitment, and the encouraging of a positive wearing society.

Social figures inside networks frequently accomplish amazing status through their imaginative articulations, be it in music, writing, or visual expressions. Inside and out investigations of these neighborhood legends give a window into the inventive strategies, motivations, and impacts that shape their work. Specialists can investigate the convergence of individual imaginative articulation and the social milieu of the local area, understanding how these figures become social envoys, communicating the goals and battles of their kin through their specialty.

An examination of nearby legends in the social circle additionally discloses the groundbreaking force of craftsmanship in cultivating local area personality and flexibility. These figures, through their innovative undertakings, add to the protection and development of social customs. By looking at their effect on neighborhood craftsmanship scenes, scientists can observe examples of social transmission, transformation, and development, giving significant experiences into the unique interaction among custom and innovation inside a local area.

Local area pioneers, frequently overlooked yet truly great individuals, assume a critical part in molding the social texture and prosperity of their territories. Top to bottom investigations of these neighborhood legends in positions of authority uncover the systems, values, and local area driven approaches that have added to their unmistakable quality. Analysts can examine the difficulties these pioneers have confronted, the drives they have advocated, and the cooperative endeavors that have moved them into amazing status inside their networks.

Concentrating on neighborhood legends in local area administration is fundamental for figuring out the elements of metro commitment, grassroots developments, and the manners by which people can impact positive change at the nearby level. By investigating the initiative styles of these figures, specialists can distil best practices, distinguish key achievement factors, and illuminate the improvement regarding authority programs custom-made to the particular necessities of various networks. Besides, understanding the commitments of nearby pioneers gives a guide to hopeful local area coordinators and pioneers trying to have an enduring effect.

Top to bottom investigations of explicit nearby legends go past simple documentation; they offer open doors for intergenerational information move. These examinations become vaults of intelligence, catching the encounters, experiences, and illustrations advanced by nearby legends all through their excursions. By safeguarding these accounts, networks guarantee that the qualities, customs, and imaginative methodologies exemplified by these figures are passed down to people in the future.

The instructive part of top to bottom investigations reaches out past the nearby local area to a more extensive crowd, permitting others to draw motivation and gain from the encounters of these neighborhood legends. Scientists, teachers, and policymakers can use the bits of knowledge acquired from these examinations to illuminate educational plans, local area improvement drives, and initiative preparation programs. The tales of neighborhood legends become a wellspring of nearby pride as well as significant assets for more extensive cultural learning and improvement.

In addition, top to bottom investigations of neighborhood legends add to the continuous discourse on variety, value, and consideration. These examinations give a stage to intensify voices that might have been generally underestimated or disregarded. By inspecting the tales of people who have broken hindrances, tested standards, and supported inclusivity, scientists add to a more nuanced comprehension of the assorted stories that comprise the social embroidery of various networks.

As people group advance and face new difficulties, the accounts of neighborhood legends offer immortal examples and motivation. Inside and out examinations permit specialists to recognize examples of versatility, flexibility, and local area union that are critical for exploring change. Whether it's the financial changes of a district, the effect of globalization, or the reactions to ecological difficulties, the stories of neighborhood legends give experiences into how networks have generally endured storms and arisen more grounded.

Moreover, with regards to urbanization and globalization, inside and out investigations of neighborhood legends become a method for saving social legacy and encouraging a feeling of spot character.

As people group go through fast changes, the tales of people who have been necessary to the texture of the region act as anchors, establishing occupants in a common history and an aggregate feeling of having a place. This association with nearby legends turns into a wellspring of strength and pride in the midst of the motion of modernization.

Nearby Legends and Their Commitments: Exploring the Woven artwork of Local area Personality

Nearby legends, those famous figures implanted in the social texture of networks, act as living narratives of shared history, strength, and motivation. These people, frequently celebrated for their accomplishments in sports, culture, or local area authority, contribute essentially to the personality and soul of their regions. In this investigation, we dive into the meaning of nearby legends and their multi-layered commitments, analyzing the manners by which their accounts explore the complex embroidery of local area character.

At the core of understanding neighborhood legends is the acknowledgment that their commitments stretch out a long ways past private accomplishments; they exemplify the goals, values, and aggregate ethos of the networks they address. These figures, whether rising up out of the domains of sports, expressions, or local area administration, become representative overseers of neighborhood character. Their accounts embody the preliminaries, wins, and exceptional stories that shape the shared awareness of their networks.

Sports, as an all inclusive language, frequently fills in as a pot for the rise of nearby legends. Inside and out investigations of competitors who achieve incredible status give a nuanced comprehension of the extraordinary force of sports inside networks. Whether it's an old neighborhood legend succeeding on the worldwide stage or a nearby group making remarkable progress, these brandishing accomplishments make a common feeling of satisfaction and solidarity. The stories of nearby games legends become meaningful of athletic ability as well as the dauntless soul that joins networks in snapshots of win.

Consider a modest community where a secondary school ball group resists the chances to bring home a state title. The headliner, frequently a neighborhood legend really taking shape, turns out to be in excess of a competitor; they address the fantasies and yearnings of a whole local area. Top to bottom investigations of such neighborhood sports legends uncover the effect of their accomplishments on local area resolve, youth commitment in sports, and the development of a culture that values discipline, collaboration, and steadiness.

Nearby legends in the social circle add to the rich woven artwork of local area personality through their imaginative undertakings. Artists, authors, visual craftsmen, and entertainers become narrators, winding around stories that reverberate with the encounters of their networks.

Top to bottom investigations of these social figures give bits of knowledge into the manners by which workmanship turns into a mirror mirroring the delights, battles, and extraordinary articulations of a local area.

Consider a people performer whose melodies catch the quintessence of provincial life, saving the practices and stories went down through ages. From the perspective of a top to bottom review, scientists can investigate how this nearby legend's music turns into a type of social protection, cultivating a profound association with legacy. The craftsman's commitments reach out past diversion; they become a social signal, enlightening the common history and values that characterize the local area.

Local area pioneers, frequently unrecognized yet truly great individuals, assume a urgent part in forming the social texture and prosperity of their regions. Top to bottom investigations of nearby legends in positions of authority uncover the techniques, values, and local area driven approaches that have added to their conspicuousness. These examinations dig into the difficulties these pioneers have confronted, the drives they have supported, and the cooperative endeavors that have pushed them into amazing status inside their networks.

The nearby entrepreneur who changes a striving area through inventive drives, the grassroots coordinator who advocates for civil rights, or the teacher who commits a lifetime to sustaining the personalities of ages — all become neighborhood legends. Top to bottom investigations of these local area pioneers give a window into the elements of city commitment, grassroots developments, and the manners by which people can impact positive change at the nearby level.

Moreover, people group pioneers frequently act as scaffolds between various sections of society, cultivating inclusivity and social union. Top to bottom examinations permit specialists to investigate how these nearby legends explore the intricacies of variety, making spaces where everybody feels seen and heard. Their commitments stretch out past their nearby authoritative reaches, making expanding influences that shape the more extensive account of local area personality.

While nearby legends rise up out of different fields, the embodiment of their commitments lies in the effect on local area attachment and the feeling of having a place. Through inside and out examinations, scientists can unload the layers of impact that these figures apply on the social, social, and profound elements of their networks. These investigations act as a demonstration of the cooperative connection between nearby legends and the networks they call home.

With regards to urbanization and globalization, neighborhood legends become urgent anchors in saving social legacy and cultivating a feeling of spot character.

As people group go through fast changes, the tales of people who have been basic to the texture of the region act as anchors, establishing occupants in a common history and an aggregate feeling of having a place. This association with nearby legends turns into a wellspring of security and pride in the midst of the motion of modernization.

In the domain of schooling, neighborhood legends frequently arise as tutors, teachers, or people who have made enduring commitments to the scholarly and self-awareness of local area individuals. Inside and out investigations of these figures give experiences into the groundbreaking force of schooling at the nearby level. These examinations might zero in on the educator who roused ages of understudies, the administrator who opened up universes of information, or the local area senior who conferred shrewdness through casual training.

Think about a nearby writer whose books, however not commonly known on a worldwide scale, have become dearest inside the local area. A top to bottom investigation of this abstract figure discloses the manners by which their words reverberate with the encounters and yearnings of neighborhood perusers. The writer's commitments stretch out past scholarly accomplishment; they become a social standard, cultivating an affection for perusing, decisive reasoning, and the festival of neighborhood stories.

Top to bottom investigations of neighborhood legends additionally shed light on the diversity of their commitments. Numerous nearby legends are not bound to a solitary space; they wear different caps, adding to the local area in different limits. For instance, a previous competitor could change into local area initiative, utilizing their impact to resolve social issues. Inside and out examinations permit specialists to investigate the interconnectedness of these jobs and the all encompassing effect nearby legends have on local area advancement.

The getting through tradition of neighborhood legends is established in the inter-generational move of information, values, and motivation. Top to bottom examinations become conductors for protecting the accounts of these figures, guaranteeing that their accounts are not lost to time. The experiences acquired from these examinations add to a more extensive comprehension of the elements that shape local area personality and the manners by which people, through their commitments, become modelers of that character.

Besides, neighborhood legends frequently act as tutors and good examples, moving the cutting edge to think ambitiously and seek to significance. Inside and out examinations give a stage to investigating the mentorship elements at play, understanding how these figures effectively add to the improvement of future pioneers, specialists, competitors, and local area manufacturers. The tales of mentorship become indispensable parts of the neighborhood legend's story, exhibiting a pledge to the constant prospering of the local area.

The accounts of nearby legends additionally hold the ability to challenge generalizations and widen viewpoints. Inside and out examinations uncover the variety of commitments inside networks and destroy assumptions about who can be a nearby legend. Whether it's a lady breaking obstructions in a male-overwhelmed field, a person with handicaps accomplishing surprising accomplishments, or an individual from an underrepresented local area making significant commitments — these accounts reclassify the forms of being a neighborhood legend.

Neighborhood legends and their commitments address a powerful interchange among people and the networks they possess. Top to bottom investigations of these figures give an all encompassing comprehension of their effect, unwinding the layers of impact that stretch out past private accomplishments. Whether in sports, culture, local area authority, or training, neighborhood legends become imperative strings in the mind boggling embroidery of local area personality. Their accounts act as reference points of motivation, social safeguarding, and impetuses for positive change. As specialists keep on investigating the diverse components of neighborhood legends, they contribute not exclusively to the documentation of individual accomplishments yet in addition to the more extensive talk on local area strength, pride, and the persevering through soul that characterizes these districts.

7.2. Exploration of their playing style, achievements, and community involvement

Investigation of Nearby Legends: Playing Style, Accomplishments, and Local area Inclusion

Nearby legends, those famous figures profoundly implanted in the social embroidered artwork of their networks, frequently accumulate recognition for their uncommon abilities as well as for their unmistakable playing styles, amazing accomplishments, and significant local area contribution. In this investigation, we dig into the nuanced aspects of these nearby legends, taking apart their playing styles, praising their accomplishments, and analyzing the significant effect of their local area contribution.

The playing style of a neighborhood legend is a characterizing part of their person-ality, frequently adding to their unbelievable status inside the local area. In sports, this style rises above simple physicality; it turns into a remarkable articulation of expertise, procedure, and character. Take, for instance, a neighborhood b-ball legend known for their energizing dunks, exact three-pointers, and unrivaled court vision. Through top to bottom investigation, specialists can analyze the complexities of their playing style, investigating the specialized ability, key splendor, and energy that put them aside.

The investigation of playing style stretches out past the actual parts of the game; it digs into the mental and profound aspects that portray a neighborhood legend's way to deal with their game.

Consider a soccer player celebrated for their quiet disposition on the field, out-standing ball control, and capacity to stay created in high-pressure circumstances. Top to bottom examinations can unwind the psychological backbone, dynamic cycles, and authority characteristics that characterize this playing style, offering bits of knowledge into the elusive components that add to their unbelievable status.

Besides, the playing style of nearby legends frequently mirrors a profound associ-ation with the social and social setting of their networks. In sports like baseball or cricket, where custom and technique entwine, a nearby legend's playing style could consolidate components that give recognition to neighborhood customs or verifiable stories. Through cautious investigation, specialists can uncover the layers of social importance woven into the texture of a nearby legend's way to deal with their game, uncovering how their playing style turns into a powerful articulation of local area personality.

Accomplishments act as unmistakable markers of a neighborhood legend's great-ness, typifying the zenith of their commitments to their individual fields. Top to bottom investigations of these accomplishments give a far reaching comprehension of the difficulties survive, records broke, and achievements accomplished. Consider a nearby olympic style events star who, despite everything, gets various gold decorations in worldwide contests. Specialists can dig into the preparation regimens, cutthroat procedures, and snapshots of win that characterize these accomplishments, unwind-ing the intricate stories that go with athletic achievement.

The investigation of accomplishments stretches out past individual honors to group achievements that add to a neighborhood legend's inheritance. In group activ-ities, nearby legends frequently assume essential parts in driving their crews to title triumphs or remarkable achievement. By analyzing these group accomplishments, specialists can reveal the cooperative elements, administration methodologies, and shared pride that support the progress of both the individual and the group. The accomplishments become markers of individual greatness as well as images of local area strength and solidarity.

In addition, the effect of neighborhood legends' accomplishments resounds a long ways past the battleground, impacting the desires and aspirations of more youthful ages inside their networks. Top to bottom examinations give a focal point through which scientists can look at the instructive, persuasive, and helpful elements of these accomplishments. For instance, a nearby swimmer who turns into the first from their local area to fit the bill for the Olympics motivates another age of youthful competitors to seek after their fantasies with enduring assurance.

The accomplishments of nearby legends additionally add to the height of local area pride and personality. Whether it's a performer getting public recognition, a craftsman exhibiting work in esteemed displays, or a researcher making notable revelations, these accomplishments become wellsprings of aggregate pride.

Scientists can investigate how the accomplishments of nearby legends reverberate with local area individuals, encouraging a feeling of having a place and building up the conviction that significance can rise up out of any edge of the local area.

Local area inclusion addresses a vital feature of a neighborhood legend's effect, as it changes their impact from the domain of sports or human expressions into a power for positive change inside the local area. Nearby legends frequently influence their foundation to offer in return, becoming bosses of worthy missions, tutors hoping for abilities, or supporters for civil rights. Through top to bottom examinations, specialists can unwind the diverse manners by which these figures effectively draw in with and add to the prosperity of their networks.

Think about a resigned competitor who, rather than pulling out from public life, lays out sports institutes, conducts youth strengthening projects, or starts local area improvement projects. Inside and out examination can reveal the inspirations, systems, and supported endeavors that describe their local area contribution. The competitor's change from the zenith of their vocation to a local area manufacturer turns into a story of flexibility, versatility, and a pledge to leaving an enduring inheritance that stretches out past the battleground.

In the domain of human expression, local area contribution could appear as nearby specialists arranging studios, making public establishments, or utilizing their foundation to resolve social issues. Through top to bottom examinations, analysts can investigate the manners by which these specialists become impetuses for social enhancement, local area discourse, and the cultivating of inventive articulation among inhabitants. Their contribution turns into a demonstration of the extraordinary force of human expressions in making dynamic and associated networks.

Local area association additionally reaches out to nearby legends in administrative roles, whether in business, training, or metro commitment. Top to bottom examinations can look at how these pioneers effectively take part in neighborhood drives, team up with local area associations, and supporter for approaches that advance inclusivity and prosperity. The neighborhood entrepreneur who focuses on feasible practices, the teacher who champions instructive value, or the urban pioneer who leads ecological preservation endeavors — all become nearby legends through their obligation to local area government assistance.

Besides, nearby legends frequently become coaches and good examples, effectively captivating with the cutting edge to support and guide arising abilities. With regards to sports, a resigned competitor could lay out mentorship programs, offering hopeful competitors admittance to preparing, counsel, and backing. Top to bottom examinations can enlighten the manners by which these mentorship drives contribute not exclusively to individual expertise improvement yet in addition to the development of a positive games culture inside the local area.

In human expression, neighborhood legends frequently take on mentorship jobs, giving direction and chances to arising craftsmen. Whether through conventional mentorship programs or casual coordinated efforts, these figures become instrumental in forming the creative scene of their networks. Specialists can investigate the guide mentee elements, revealing insight into the persevering through effect of these connections on the development and variety of inventive articulations inside the local area.

In people group administration, mentorship and local area contribution remain closely connected. Nearby pioneers frequently devote time to coach arising pioneers, sharing bits of knowledge, giving systems administration open doors, and bestowing significant examples from their own encounters. Inside and out investigations can disentangle the far reaching influences of this mentorship, displaying how it adds to the improvement of a hearty initiative pipeline inside the local area.

The investigation of neighborhood legends and their commitments is inadequate without recognizing the advantageous connection between the individual and the local area. Neighborhood legends are not made in disconnection; they are molded by the qualities, emotionally supportive networks, and extraordinary elements of the networks they hail from. Alternately, neighborhood legends add to the advancement of these networks, becoming main thrusts for positive change and social improvement.

Nearby legends, through their playing styles, accomplishments, and local area inclusion, become living exemplifications of the goals and flexibility of their networks. Top to bottom investigations give a focal point through which specialists can examine the unpredictable interchange between individual greatness and shared character. Whether on the games field, in the social circle, or inside local area administration, neighborhood legends explore the intricacies of their jobs with a significant comprehension of the effect they employ.

In the realm of sports, neighborhood legends stand apart for their amazing accomplishments as well as for the particular playing styles that have become inseparable from their names. These playing styles are not simple presentations of physicality; they are extraordinary articulations of expertise, methodology, and character that put these figures aside and add to their famous status inside their networks.

Consider a neighborhood ball legend known for their charging dunks, exact three-pointers, and unmatched court vision. An inside and out examination of their playing style would dive into the specialized subtleties of their moves, the essential splendor behind their choices on the court, and the pizazz that enamors fans. It goes past the actual ability, taking advantage of the mental and close to home aspects that describe how they approach the game. This unmistakable playing style turns into a characterizing part of their personality, making an association with fans that rises above the limits of the games field.

In group activities, the playing style of neighborhood legends frequently stretches out to their positions of authority inside the group. A soccer commander, for example, may be commended for their singular abilities as well as for their capacity to coordinate plays, rouse colleagues, and stay created in high-pressure circumstances. The top to bottom investigation of their playing style uncovers the specialized parts of their game as well as the elusive characteristics that make them compelling pioneers on and off the field. It turns into a concentrate in essential brightness, collaboration, and the exemplification of the qualities that resound with their local area.

Accomplishments act as substantial achievements that mark the zenith of a nearby legend's vocation. These achievements go past private greatness; they become images of strength, commitment, and the quest for significance. Whether it's an olympic style events star getting different gold decorations in global rivalries or a nearby ball club securing a notable title triumph, these accomplishments add to the legend's heritage and make a permanent imprint on the local area.

Top to bottom investigations of these accomplishments give an extensive comprehension of the difficulties survive, records broke, and achievements accomplished. Analysts dig into the preparation regimens, serious techniques, and snapshots of win that characterize these achievements. The account of these accomplishments turns into an account of persistence, vital splendor, and the resolute obligation to arriving at new levels. Besides, in group activities, the aggregate accomplishments add to a common feeling of satisfaction and character inside the local area.

The effect of neighborhood legends' accomplishments stretches out a long ways past the battleground. These achievements act as wellsprings of motivation for more youthful ages inside their networks. A neighborhood swimmer turning into the first from their local area to fit the bill for the Olympics, for instance, motivates another age of youthful competitors to seek after their fantasies earnestly. Inside and out examinations can investigate the instructive, persuasive, and optimistic elements of these accomplishments, revealing insight into how they add to the improvement of local area individuals and ingrain a feeling of plausibility.

Moreover, accomplishments become markers of local area pride and personality. Whether it's a performer getting public recognition, a craftsman exhibiting work in renowned displays, or a researcher making notable revelations, these achievements hoist the local area on a more extensive stage. Specialists can investigate how the accomplishments of neighborhood legends resound with local area individuals, cultivating a feeling of having a place and supporting the conviction that significance can rise up out of any edge of the local area.

The investigation of playing style and accomplishments of neighborhood legends gives a nuanced comprehension of these notorious figures inside their networks. Past the insights and awards, it digs into the quintessence of their way to deal with their separate fields, uncovering the complexities of their playing styles.

All the while, it commends the substantial achievements that represent their greatness and add to the aggregate character of the local area. As specialists proceed to take apart and investigate these angles, they contribute not exclusively to the documentation of individual heritages yet in addition to the more extensive account of local area flexibility, pride, and the persevering through soul that characterizes these districts.

7.3. Personal anecdotes and interviews with players, coaches, and community members

Individual stories and meetings with players, mentors, and local area individuals give a rich embroidery of bits of knowledge into the lives, encounters, and effect of neighborhood legends. These stories offer a refining focal point through which we can grasp the singular excursions, difficulties, and wins that add to the incredible status of these figures inside their networks.

Setting out on an excursion through private tales delivers the cozy subtleties of a nearby legend's life, revealing insight into the developmental encounters that formed their personality and powered their goals. Envision hearing the youth accounts of a darling competitor who originally found their energy for the game while playing in the local roads. These stories divulge the early impacts, familial help, and the sheer happiness that lighted their excursion toward turning into a nearby legend.

Top to bottom meetings with players dig into the complexities of their playing styles, giving a firsthand record of the manners of thinking, techniques, and close to home aspects that characterize their way to deal with the game. A ball player might relate the invigoration of making a game-dominating shot or the strength expected to return from a vocation compromising injury. Through these meetings, scientists get sufficiently close to the internal functions of a player's outlook, disclosing the psychological backbone, devotion, and love for the game that support their unbelievable status.

Mentors, frequently instrumental figures in the advancement of neighborhood legends, contribute special points of view on the groundbreaking excursions of their players. Their stories might rotate around the difficulties of supporting crude ability, ingraining discipline, and cultivating a feeling of collaboration. A meeting with a mentor could uncover the vital minutes when they perceived the uncommon possible in a youthful competitor or the essential choices that impelled their group to title triumphs. These stories become strings in the more extensive account of mentorship, direction, and the cooperative endeavors that shape the ascent of nearby legends.

Local area individuals, seeing the effect of neighborhood legends firsthand, offer an aggregate voice that repeats the opinions, pride, and shared encounters inside the territory. Individual stories from fans who recollect the jolting air of a title game, the fervor of a social exhibition, or the extraordinary impact of a nearby pioneer give an all encompassing point of view.

Interviews with local area individuals catch the reverberation of a nearby legend's accomplishments inside the social texture, underlining the job these figures play in cultivating local area union and pride.

Consider a nearby performer whose exhibitions at local area occasions have become valued customs. Individual accounts from crowd individuals could ponder the profound association produced through the music, the social meaning of the craftsman's work, and the feeling of solidarity experienced during live exhibitions. Interviews with local area individuals could disclose how the performer's imaginativeness has turned into a wellspring of motivation, encouraging a common character and reinforcing the securities inside the local area.

These individual accounts additionally feature the difficulties nearby legends explore on their ways to significance. A competitor might share accounts of steadiness through wounds, the penances made to seek after their energy, or the flexibility expected to defeat difficulties. Interviews with mentors might uncover the essential choices made during crucial points in time of misfortune, exhibiting the job of administration in directing groups through difficulties. These tales acculturate the legends, making their accounts engaging and rousing for local area individuals confronting their own preliminaries.

Inside and out interviews with neighborhood legends themselves offer a stage for thoughtfulness, permitting them to consider their excursions, inspirations, and the effect of their commitments. A soccer player could share the profound load of addressing their local area on a global stage or the extraordinary impact of sports in forming their personality. The performer might relate the development of their imaginative voice, the social stories implanted in their work, and the obligation they feel as a social minister. These meetings become gateways into the personalities of neighborhood legends, giving scientists a more profound comprehension of the individual aspects that fuel their obligation to greatness.

Individual tales and meetings additionally enlighten the complementary connection between nearby legends and their networks. For example, a nearby entrepreneur who rejuvenates an area might share tales of the local area individuals who motivated their drives, the cooperative endeavors with neighborhood occupants, and the common feeling of responsibility in the renewal cycle. These stories underline the cooperative idea of the connection between nearby legends and the networks they serve, building up the possibility that significance is many times developed inside the aggregate yearnings of a territory.

Besides, interviews with nearby legends offer a chance to investigate their local area association past the domain of their essential accomplishments. The resigned competitor who lays out local area programs, the craftsman who starts social drives, or the business chief who champions neighborhood causes — all offer bits of knowledge into the inspirations and procedures behind their local area commitment.

Individual stories from these figures might uncover the significant effect of offering in return, the delight got from sustaining the future, and the feeling of obligation that accompanies being a nonentity inside the local area.

In the domain of sports, individual tales frequently weave accounts of brotherhood, cooperation, and the bonds produced on and off the battleground. Interviews with players could reveal the companionships that rise above rivalry, the mentorship elements with partners, and the common triumphs that become permanent recollections. Mentors, in their appearance, may share the pride in seeing players develop as competitors as well as people who contribute genuinely to the local area.

These individual stories likewise give a window into the groundbreaking force of sports as an impetus for social change. Consider a soccer player who, through their own tales, relates how the game turned into a vehicle for advancing inclusivity, stalling social obstructions, and cultivating solidarity inside a different local area. Interviews with local area individuals could uncover the far reaching influences of sports drives, displaying how neighborhood legends influence their impact to set out open doors, rouse youth, and impart a deep satisfaction.

In artistic expression, individual accounts from performers, visual specialists, or scholars might uncover the snapshots of imaginative disclosure, the impacts that shape their inventive articulations, and the convergence of their work with the social milieu of their networks. Meetings might dive into the craftsman's job in protecting social customs, testing cultural standards, or utilizing their foundation to enhance underrepresented voices. These individual stories become windows into the spirit of the craftsman, catching the energy, weakness, and cultural reflections implanted in their work.

Local area pioneers, through private stories and meetings, share accounts of administration, support, and the cooperative endeavors that add to positive local area results. Stories from a nearby pioneer could describe the grassroots drives that address squeezing local area issues, the organizations produced with inhabitants, and the essential choices made to impact positive change. Interviews offer bits of knowledge into the pioneer's inspirations, the difficulties looked in local area work, and the persevering through obligation to making a comprehensive and flourishing territory.

The intergenerational effect of nearby legends comes to the very front through private accounts and meetings with the individuals who have straightforwardly profited from their mentorship. Consider the hopeful competitor who shares stories of the direction got from a neighborhood legend, the craftsman who ponders the groundbreaking impact of a coach, or the local area pioneer who credits their obligation to administration to the motivation drawn from a nonentity. These individual stories become tributes to the persevering through tradition of nearby legends, accentuating their job as coaches and draftsmen of future local area pioneers.

Interviews with players and mentors offer a significant look into the unpredictable elements of sports, uncovering the individual stories, vital bits of knowledge, and groundbreaking encounters that shape neighborhood legends inside their networks. These discussions with the critical heroes of the donning story give an exceptional point of view that rises above measurements and honors, permitting us to investigate the human components of physicality, mentorship, and local area influence.

Starting with players, interviews reveal the mind boggling embroidery of their playing styles, inspirations, and the profound rollercoaster that characterizes a lifelong in sports. Picture a b-ball player whose mark continues on the court have turned into a wellspring of wonder for fans. Through interviews, we get to the player's manners of thinking during crucial points in time, the essential choices that support their way to deal with the game, and the profound ups and downs that go with every triumph and rout.

A ball player, for example, could ponder the impacts that molded their playing style — the patio games that touched off their enthusiasm, the mentors who leveled up their abilities, and the pivotal turning points that cemented their character on the court. These individual bits of knowledge give specialists a more profound comprehension of the human behind the competitor, digging into the inspirations that fuel their obligation to greatness and the job of sports in forming their personality.

Besides, interviews with players unwind the immaterial characteristics that characterize a neighborhood legend's effect in the group and local area. The kinship with colleagues, the mentorship elements inside the storage space, and the cooperative endeavors that lead to triumph become focal subjects. For example, a soccer player might share stories of the implicit bonds produced on the field, the common triumphs that make getting through recollections, and the initiative illustrations gained from being important for a durable group.

Past the battleground, interviews permit players to think about their job as local area diplomats. A neighborhood legend might examine the obligations that accompany being a good example for trying competitors, the delight got from local area commitment, and the effect of sports in encouraging solidarity. These accounts become tributes to the groundbreaking force of sports in molding individual vocations as well as the social texture of the networks they address.

Mentors, frequently instrumental in the improvement of nearby legends, offer an extraordinary viewpoint that joins vital keenness, mentorship, and a significant comprehension of the human part of sports. Interviews with mentors dive into their instructing ways of thinking, the difficulties of supporting ability, and the essential choices that characterize a group's prosperity. The ball mentor, for example, may share bits of knowledge into the improvement of a headliner, the essential moves that solid vital triumphs, and the mentorship elements that stretch out past the court.

Mentors become narrators, winding around stories of versatility, discipline, and the essential brightness expected to direct a group to triumph. Interviews give a stage to mentors to ponder the snapshots of motivation that characterize their instructing vocations — the forward leaps with players, the difficulties survive, and the pride got from seeing competitors develop into neighborhood legends. These discussions refine the training experience, accentuating the multifaceted dance among procedure and mentorship that adds to the development of donning greatness.

Also, interviews with mentors offer experiences into the cooperative connection among tutor and competitor. A soccer mentor, for instance, could describe the excursion of a player from their initial days in the young foundation to turning into a star on the public stage. These stories feature the job of training in refining specialized abilities as well as supporting the person, flexibility, and initiative characteristics that characterize a neighborhood legend.

The essential choices made during crucial points in time become central focuses in interviews with mentors. The baseball trainer, pondering a title winning season, could dig into the game-changing strategies utilized, the persuasive systems utilized during testing periods, and the cooperative endeavors that characterize a fruitful instructing vocation. These meetings furnish specialists with bits of knowledge into the complex components of instructing, rising above the Xs and operating system to investigate the ability to understand people on a profound level, initiative, and mentorship at the core of the training venture.

The effect of mentors reaches out past the battleground, with interviews uncovering the obligation to local area advancement and the mentorship drives that stretch out past games. A mentor could examine the foundation of youth programs, the accentuation on all encompassing turn of events, and the pride got from seeing competitors prevail in sports as well as contribute genuinely to their networks. These discussions become windows into the groundbreaking impact mentors use, as tacticians as well as designers of character and local area commitment.

Besides, interviews with the two players and mentors give a comprehensive comprehension of the complex connections that characterize the brandishing environment. The common stories of difficulties, triumphs, and cooperative endeavors become strings in the more extensive embroidered artwork of sports culture. Consider a b-ball player and their mentor pondering the critical minutes that characterized their title winning season — the common victories, the essential choices made pair, and the implicit comprehension that describes a fruitful player-mentor dynamic.

These meetings additionally shed light on the mentorship elements at play, displaying the persevering through influence mentors have on the individual and expert advancement of competitors. A hopeful competitor might share tales of the direction got, the extraordinary impact of a mentor's mentorship, and the illustrations that stretch out past the battleground. Interviews become courses for investigating the intergenerational move of information, accentuating the job of guides in molding the directions of future nearby legends.

Individual tales inside interviews frequently become powerful reflections on flexibility, conquering misfortune, and the immovable obligation to one's energy. A soccer player might describe the difficulties looked in their initial profession, the snapshots of self-question, and the vital choices that moved them to turn into a nearby legend. Mentors could share accounts of remaking seasons, the essential turns made during testing periods, and the significant fulfillment got from seeing competitors vanquish individual and aggregate obstructions.

The refining impact of these accounts reaches out to the more extensive local area, where fans and occupants become vital narrators. Local area individuals, through interviews, articulate the close to home association they feel to neighborhood legends — the common delight of triumph, the aggregate distress of rout, and the motivation drawn from seeing their accomplishments. These individual stories add to the common story, stressing the job of neighborhood legends in cultivating a common personality and pride inside the territory.

Besides, interviews give a stage to local area individuals to communicate the groundbreaking impact of neighborhood legends past the games field. Consider a performer whose exhibitions at local area occasions have become esteemed customs. Interviews with crowd individuals could catch the profound reverberation of the music, the social meaning of the craftsman's work, and the feeling of solidarity experienced during live exhibitions. These stories feature the sweeping effect of nearby legends in the social and social elements of a local area.

Top to bottom meetings with local area individuals likewise deliver points of view on the local area contribution of nearby legends. A nearby entrepreneur, through private tales, could share accounts of local area drives, coordinated efforts with inhabitants, and the essential choices made to contribute decidedly to the area. These accounts become tributes to the interconnectedness between neighborhood legends and the networks they serve, underlining the common obligation regarding local area prosperity.

Interviews with players, mentors, and local area individuals offer a diverse investigation of the lives, accomplishments, and effect of nearby legends. These individual stories give a nuanced comprehension of the human components of sports, rising above measurements to catch the substance of physicality, mentorship, and local area commitment. As specialists dig into the rich embroidery of individual stories, they contribute not exclusively to the documentation of individual heritages yet additionally to the more extensive story of local area flexibility, motivation, and the getting through soul that nearby legends bring to the different territories they call home.

Printed in the USA
CPSIA information can be obtained
at www.ICGtesting.com
LVHW010105270124
769490LV00080B/3109